Clive James was educated at Sydney University and at Cambridge, where he was president of Footlights. In addition to his bestseller *Unreliable Memoirs* and his novel *Brilliant Creatures*, he has published four mock-epic poems, *The Fate of Felicity Fark, Peregrine Prykke's Pilgrimage, Britannia Bright's Bewilderment*, and *Charles Charming's Challenges*; three books of literary criticism, *The Metropolitan Critic, At the Pillars of Hercules* and *From the Land of Shadows* (which is available in Picador); a book of verse letters, *Fan-Mail*, and a verse diary, *Poem of the Year*. Between 1972 and 1982 he was television critic for the *Observer*. The three volumes of selections from his column are entitled *Visions Before Midnight, The Crystal Bucket* and *Glued to the Box* (all of which are available in Picador). His travel writings appear in a volume *Flying Visits – Postcards from the Observer 1979–1983* (also in Picador). As a television performer he has appeared regularly in several series, most notably 'Cinema', 'Saturday Night People', 'Clive James on Television' and 'The Late Clive James'. His television documentaries include 'Paris Fashion Show' and 'Live in Las Vegas'.

Clive James

FALLING TOWARDS ENGLAND
Unreliable Memoirs II

PICADOR

published by Pan Books
in association with Jonathan Cape

First published 1985 by Jonathan Cape Ltd
This Picador edition published 1986 by Pan Books Ltd,
Cavaye Place, London SW10 9PG
9 8 7 6
© Clive James 1985
ISBN 0 330 29437 7
Printed and bound in Great Britain by
Cox & Wyman Ltd, Reading

To Chester and John Cummings

I had already noticed with various people that the affectation of praiseworthy sentiments is not the only way of covering up reprehensible ones, but that a more up-to-date method is to put these latter on exhibition, so that one has the air of at least being forthright.

Proust, *Le Temps retrouvé*

All censure of a man's self is oblique praise. It is in order to show how much he can spare.

Johnson

Contents

Preface

This is the second volume of my unreliable memoirs. For a palpable fantasy, the first volume was well enough received. It purported to be the true story of how the author grew from infancy through adolescence to early manhood, this sequence of amazing biological developments largely taking place in Kogarah, a suburb of Sydney, NSW, Australia. And indeed it *was* a true story, in the sense that I wasn't brought up in a Tibetan monastery or a castle on the Danube. The central character was something like my real self. If the characters around him were composites, they were obviously so, and with some justification. The friend who helps you dig tunnels in your back yard is rarely the same friend who ruins your summer by flying a model aeroplane into your mother's prize trifle, but a book with everybody in it would last as long as life, and never live at all.

As for the adults, they were shadows, but that was true to how children see, and my mother, in particular, was too much of an influence on my life for me to appreciate at that age – or at any subsequent age, for that matter. Her quiet but strenuous objections to *Unreliable Memoirs* arose from my depiction, not of her, but of myself. Apparently I was not the near-delinquent portrayed, but a little angel: to suggest otherwise reflected badly on her. The insult was not meant. Perhaps I should have pointed out more often that without her guidance and example I might have gone straight from short pants to Long Bay Gaol, which in those days was still in use and heavily populated by larcenous young men who had chosen their parents less wisely.

Unlike my mother and my father, who were robbed by history of a rounding to their youth, I had come peacefully to my middle years and wanted to celebrate my good luck, or at any rate atone for it, by evoking a childhood blessed enough to be typical. But the typical, for even the most high-minded male child, does not exclude the revolting. I tried to leave some of that in. One might argue that I should have made a more thorough job of it. A Scots lady ninety-three years old sent me a charming letter saying that when young in Ayrshire she had done all the things I did. The book must have been read aloud to her, by someone who knew which pages to pass over in silence.

To tell my story in the belief that I was remarkable would have been sufficiently conceited. To tell it in the hope of being universal was possibly even more conceited, not to say pretentious. He who abandons his claim to be unique is even less bearable when he claims to be representative. But at least he has *tried* to climb down. There is a story by Schnitzler, called 'History of a Genius', about a butterfly so impressed by how far it has come in one day that it resolves to dictate its autobiography. Yet Schnitzler, so greatly generous about human beings, sells the butterfly short. The butterfly's only mistake is to imagine itself unusual. The story of its day would be well worth having, and all the more so if it realised that millions of its fellows shared the same career. Usual does not mean ordinary. A butterfly's compound eyes, which can see in the infra-red, are no less extraordinary because every other butterfly has them. The same applies to human memory. When I hold my hands as if in prayer and roll a pencil between them, I can smell the plasticine snakes I made in Class 1B at Kogarah Infants' School. There is nothing ordinary about that.

Far from being all done in a day, my own story is of a late developer: one who, deficient in natural wisdom, has had to learn everything by trial and error. In this book my errors continue, but in a different context. In Sydney I had come of age but still had a lot to learn. In Europe I forgot what little I knew. London in the Sixties, it was generally believed, had sprung to life. Lost somewhere in the hubbub, I either marked time or went backwards. Readers who grew up faster, wherever they did so, might still recognise in these pages something of what they went through in order to become what they now are. Those whose personalities were handed to them in one piece might shake their heads. There are such people, and often they are among the saints, but they are denied the salutary privilege of remembering what they once were, before they knew better. It is possible that they are also denied knowledge of where the human comedy begins, in the individual soul. But I wouldn't want to be caught suggesting that the past dissolves in mirth. Things happen that can't be laughed off. Our hero is a bit older in this book, and the same ways are not necessarily so winning.

Not that I have registered here the full squalor of my past derelictions, some of which I can't begin to recall without an involuntary yell to quash the memory. But to confess would be an indulgence, and there are bigger sinners growing old in Paraguay. Young Australian men living in London drank a great deal but broke nothing except the hearts of young Australian women. Feminism as a mass movement was imminent but had not yet arrived; women were still exploitable; and men duly exploited them. For the sons of the Anzacs this wasn't a very noble chapter, and the girls who suffered, should they read this book twenty years later, might justly complain that I have glossed it over. For them to know that the crassness of their young men was waiting for them at home was bad enough, without encountering more of the same when they arrived abroad. Some of them might find their faintest outlines here, sharing a false name, catching someone else's bus to work in Lambeth or Fulham. No disrespect is intended: quite the opposite. The full complexity of the human personality is something I no longer presume to sum up, or even to suggest.

I can't remember having been *consciously* insensitive. I can hardly remember being consciously anything, except cold. It was all a bit like being on the Moon: you moved forward because you were falling forward. The clear path is revealed later, looking back. Which doesn't mean that one disclaims responsibility for one's actions. We are what we have done; and besides, we can't deny it without giving up our pride. 'For my part, since I have always admitted that I was the chief cause of all the misfortunes which have befallen me,' wrote Casanova in his old age, 'I have rejoiced in my ability to be my own pupil, and in my duty to love my teacher.' Did knowing himself to be vain make him less vain? Leaving the metaphysics to others, he died writing his life story – which, considering the other things he might have died doing, was not the least dignified way he could have gone. What a swathe he would have cut through Kogarah! A thought to keep the reader's expectations in proportion as I begin this account of my impact on England, drawn there by gravity like a snowflake to the ground.

London, 1985   C. J.

I

Soft Landing

When we got off the ship in Southampton in that allegedly
mild January of 1962 I had nothing to declare at customs
except goose-pimples under my white nylon drip-dry
shirt. This was not because I had been prudent in my
spending but because I had spent the last of my money
in Singapore, plus twenty pounds I had borrowed from
one of my cabin mates – and which I still owe him, come
to think of it. The money had gone on a new suit which
I didn't actually have with me in my luggage. The tailors
in Singapore's Change Alley had taken my measurements
and promised to send the finished suit after me to London.
This had seemed like a sensible arrangement, so I had
handed over the cash, thereby depriving myself of any
leeway for a spending spree later on in Aden. I thus
missed out on the chance, seized by most of the other
Australians of my own age on the ship, to be guided by
the expertise of Arab salesmen in the purchase of German
tape-recorders and Japanese cameras at a fraction of the
price – something like five-fourths – prevailing in their
countries of origin.

In the crater of Aden, while my compatriots knowingly
examined the Arabic guarantee forms for machines
whose batteries were mysteriously unavailable, I hovered
in the heat-hazed background, sullenly attempting not to
catch the remaining eye of a beggar whose face had

otherwise been entirely chewed off by a camel. It had been very hot in Aden. In England it was very cold: colder than I had ever known. The customs men did a great deal of heavy-handed chaffing about how you cobbers couldn't really call this a winter, ho ho, and what we would look like if there really was a winter, har har, and so on. Their accents were far funnier than their sense of humour. They all seemed to have stepped out of the feature list of an Ealing comedy for the specific purpose of unpacking our luggage and charging us extra for everything in it. My own luggage consisted mainly of one very large suitcase made of mock leather – i.e., real cardboard. This compendium was forced into rotundity by a valuable collection of tennis shorts, running shorts, Hawaiian shirts, T-shirts, Hong Kong thong rubber sandals, short socks, sandshoes and other apparel equally appropriate for an English winter. The customs officer sifted through the heap twice, the second time looking at me instead of at it, as if my face would betray the secret of the illicit fortunes to be made by smuggling unsuitable clothing across half the world.

As the people all around me were presented with huge bills, I gave silent thanks for being in possession of nothing assessable for duty. The ship's fool – a pimply, bespectacled British emigrant called Tanner who was now emigrating back the other way – was near tears. In Aden and Port Said he had bought, among other things, two tape recorders, a Japanese camera called something like a Naka-mac with a silver box full of lenses, a portable television set slightly larger than an ordinary domestic model but otherwise no different except that it had a handle, a stuffable leather television pouffe for watching it from, a hi-fi outfit with separate components, and a pair of binoculars so powerful that it frightened you to look through them, especially if you saw Tanner. Most of this gear he had about his person, although some of it was packed in large cardboard boxes, because all this was happening in the days before miniaturisation, when an amplifier still had valves. The customs officer calculated the duty owing and confronted him with the total, at which he sat down on his boxed telescope and briefly wept. It was more money than he had in the world, so he just signed away the whole mountain of gear and walked on through a long door in the far side of the shed.

A few minutes afterwards I walked through the same door and emerged in England, where it was gently snowing on to a bus full of Australians. There was a small cloud in front of my face which I quickly deduced to be my breath. The bus was provided by the Overseas Visitors' Club, known for short as the OVC. The journey by ship, the bus ride to London and a week of bed and breakfast in Earls Court were all part of the deal, which a few years later would have been called a Package, but at that time was still known as a Scheme. The general thrust of the Scheme was to absorb some of the culture shock, thus rendering it merely benumbing instead of fatal. As the bus, which strangely insisted on calling itself a coach, headed north – or west or east or wherever it was going, except, presumably, south – I looked out into the English landscape and felt glad that I had not been obliged to find my way through it unassisted.

The cars seemed very small, with no overhang at either end. A green bus had 'Green Line' written on it and could therefore safely be assumed to be a Green Line bus, or coach. The shops at the side of the road looked as if they were finely detailed painted accessories for an unusually elaborate Hornby Dublo model railway tabletop layout. Above all, as well as around all and beyond all, was the snow, almost exactly resembling the snow that fell in English films on top of people like Alastair Sim and Margaret Rutherford. What I was seeing was a familiar landscape made strange by being actual instead of transmitted through cultural intermediaries. It was a deeply unsettling sensation, which everybody else in the coach must have shared, because for the first time in twelve thousand miles there was a prolonged silence. Then one of the wits explained that the whole roadside façade would fold down after we had roared by, to reveal factories manufacturing rust-prone chromium trim for the Standard Vanguard. There was some nervous laughter and the odd confident assurance that we were already in the outskirts of London. Since the outskirts of London were well known to embrace pretty well everywhere in the south of England up to the outskirts of Birmingham, this seemed a safe bet.

A few ploughed fields presented themselves so that the girls, still pining for members of the ship's crew, might heave a chorus of long sighs at the bunny rabbits zipping across the pinwhale corduroy snow. After that it was one continuous built-up area turning to streetlight in the gathering darkness of what my watch told me was only mid-afternoon. Enveloped in many layers of clothing, people thronging the footpaths seemed to be black, brown or, if white and male, to have longer hair than the females. High to the left of an arching flyover shone the word WIMPEY, a giant, lost, abstract adjective carved from radioactive ruby.

There was no way of telling, when we arrived, that the place we were getting off at was called Earls Court. In those days it was still nicknamed Kangaroo Valley but there were no obvious signs of Australia except the foyer of the OVC, crowded with young men whose jug ears stuck out unmistakably from their short haircuts on either side of a freckled area of skin which could be distinguished as a face, rather than a neck, only by the presence of a nose and a mouth. Here I was relieved to find out that I had been assigned to the same dormitory room as my cabin mates, at a hostel around the corner. So really we were still on board ship, the journey from the OVC foyer around the corner to the hostel being the equivalent of a brisk turn around the deck, while carrying a large suitcase.

The snow was falling thickly enough to replenish a half-inch layer on the footpath, so that my black Julius Marlowe shoes could sink in slightly and, I was interested to notice, be fairly rapidly made wet. It hadn't occurred to me that snow would have this effect. I had always assumed snow to be some form of solid. In the hostel I counted up my financial resources. They came to just a bit more than ten pounds in English money. Ten pounds bought quite a lot at that time, when eight pounds a week was a labourer's living wage and you could get a bar of chocolate for threepence, a chunky hexagonal coin which I at first took to be some form of washer and then spent a lot of time standing on its edge on the bedside table while figuring out what to do next. Improvising brilliantly, I took some of the small amount of money over and above the ten pounds and invested in an aerogramme, which I converted into a begging letter and addressed to my mother, back there in Sydney with no telephone. Her resources being far from limitless, I did my best not to make the letter too heartrending, but after it was finished, folded and sealed I had to leave it on the radiator for the tears to dry out, after which it was wrinkled and dimpled like an azure poppadum.

Dinner in the hostel made me miss the ship-board menu, which until then I would have sworn nothing ever could. What on earth did a spotted dick look like before the custard drowned it? A glass mug of brown water was provided which we were assured was beer. I sipped fitfully at mine while everybody else watched. When I showed no signs of dengue fever or botulism, they tried theirs. Having rolled inaccurately into my bunk, I dis-covered, like my two cabin mates, that I couldn't sleep for the silence of the engines.

Next day there was still a tendency to cling together. I was in a three-man expedition that set out to find

Piccadilly Circus by following a map of the Underground railway system, starting at Earls Court station. To reach the station we had to travel some way on the surface, keeping a wary eye out for hostile natives. It was a relief to find that in daylight at any rate a sizeable part of the local population was Australian. At that time the Earls Court Australians had not yet taken to carrying twelve-packs of Foster's lager, and the broad-brimmed Akubra hat with corks dangling from the brim was never to be more than a myth, but there was no mistaking those open, freckled, eyeless faces, especially when they were sticking out of the top of navy-blue English duffle-coats religiously acquired as a major concession towards blend-ing into the scenery. My own duffle-coat was bright yellow in colour and would not have helped me blend into anything except a sand dune, but luckily it was hanging in my cupboard back in Kogarah, Sydney. Or unluckily, if you considered how cold I felt in my light-green sports coat with the blue fleck. Or would have felt, if I had been less excited. But we were going down in a lift through a hole in the ground to another hole in the ground which would take us under London to Piccadilly Circus. Piccadilly! I even knew what it meant. It was a tailor's term, something to do with sleeves. No doubt the tailors had started a circus when times got tough.

Knowingness evaporated when the tube train pulled into the station. The train was so small that for a moment I thought it was a toy – another component of the Hornby Dublo table-top layout, except this time under the table. You almost had to bend your head getting into it. The electric trains in Sydney were sensibly provided with four feet of spare headroom in case any visiting American basketballer wanted to hitch a ride without taking off his stilts. He might have stood out because of his colour, but at least he wouldn't be bent over double. In this train he would be bent over double, but at least he wouldn't stand out because of his colour. Half the people in the crowded carriage seemed to be black or dark brown. They were dressed just the same as the white people and often conspicuously better. I had entered my first multiracial society, all for the price of a tube ticket. If I had come from an apartheid country, I would have had a kit of reflexes that I could have set about modifying. But coming from a monotone dominion whose Aborigines were still thought of, at that time, as something between a sideshow and an embarrassment, I had nothing to go on except a blank feeling which I hoped was receptivity. A sperm whale feeding on a field of squid – not giant squid, just those little squidlets that form its basic diet – cruises along with its mouth open, taking everything in. That was me, open-mouthed to new experience. The sperm whale looks the same when drowning, of course: going down and down with its gob wide open and the pressure building up and up. By Knightsbridge we were making nervous jokes about a journey to the centre of the earth. The escalators leading to the surface at Piccadilly were like sets from *Things to Come*. Then we popped out of the ground and stood rooted to the mushy pavement by the Sheer Englishness of it all. 'Coca-Cola' said a wall of neon, glowing as if day were night – a fair assessment of the overcast morning.

But Eros was sufficiently evocative all by himself and we set off for Buckingham Palace with high hearts, going by way of Nelson's Column and the Admiralty Arch. The Mall showed pink through the churned slush, St James's Park was a spun-sugar cake-scape with clockwork ducks, and a flag on the Palace indicated that She was at home. The Guard obligingly began to change itself just as we arrived, the Coldstreams handing over to the Grenadiers. Tourism was still under control at that time so it was possible to catch the odd glimpse of the participating soldiers, instead of, as now, seeing nothing except the rear view of Norwegians carrying full camping apparatus and holding up cameras to fire blind over the hulking back-packs of other Norwegians standing in front of them. Needless to say we did not regard ourselves as tourists. Whatever our convictions, we were children of the Commonwealth, not to say the Empire. One of us rather embarrassingly stood to attention. It was not myself, since I was a radical socialist at the time, but I understood. It was something emotional that went back to Chad Valley tin toys, Brock fireworks and the every-second-Christmas box of W. Britains lead soldiers. I remembered my set of Household Cavalry with the right arms that swivelled and the swords held upright, except for the troop leader whose sabre stuck out in line with his extended arm while his horse pranced. When his arm worked loose and fell off I wodged it back on with a gasket of cigarette paper. I can remember remembering this while the band played 'British Grenadiers', and can remember how wet my eyes were, mainly from the cold that was creeping upward from my feet. At first they had been numb. Now they felt like something Scott of the Antarctic might have made a worried note about in his diary if I had been a member of his expedition. As the officers on parade screamed at each other nose to nose from under their forward-tilting bearskins, it began occurring to me that the climate was going to be a problem.

Or part of a larger problem, that of money. There was more sightseeing in the next few days, with the National Gallery putting everything else in perspective. Indeed it put its own contents into perspective, since here again, even more strikingly, there was a discrepancy between the actual and what had been made familiar in reproduction. The Rokeby Venus, for example, was supposed to be the size of half a page in a quarto art book, not as big as the serving window of Harry's Café de Wheels at Woolloomooloo. She looked a bit murky at that stage – they cleaned her a few years later, and perhaps overdid it – but her subtly dimpled bottom, poised at the height of the viewer's eyes, made you wonder about Velázquez's professional detachment. Though most of the rooms in the gallery were still a mystery to me, I was confident enough, or ignorant enough, to decide that Art with a capital 'A' was going to be a source of sensual gratification on all levels. At the Tate Gallery I was relieved to find that the Paul Klee pictures were roughly the same size as in the books. But just to reach the galleries by tube was costing money, and meanwhile time was running out.

There was a grand total of eight pounds left and it didn't help when I lost the lot, along with my prize yellow pig-skin wallet, at Waldo Laidlaw's wedding party. Arriving out of the sky in his usual grand style – absolutely nobody else you knew could afford to fly – Waldo instantly married one of the girls from my ship. Apparently it had all been arranged back in Australia. The party was in the as-yet-unfurnished shell of a ground-floor flat in that part of Camden Town where you could overlook Regent's Park if you could find your way on to the roof. In Waldo's words, overlooking it was easy, because you couldn't see it. All the Australian advertising types were there, the women unattainably well-groomed and the men sporting Chelsea boots, an elastic-sided form of footwear I had not previously encountered. I was the only one dressed for the Australian summer, with three T-shirts and a pair of running shorts on under my Hawaiian shirt and poplin trousers. Feeling the heat of the crowded room, I took off my jacket, left it in the bedroom on the bed with the overcoats, and prepared to dance.

A hit record called 'Let's Twist Again' was playing over and over. Several people among the sophisticated throng had already reached exhibition standard in dancing the Twist. I think I could have matched them through sheer inspiration, but my shoes were in bad shape and tended to stick where they were, cruelly restricting my rate and radius of swivel. In the kitchen there were big tins of brown water you could open with your thumb. I treated the stuff with the contempt it deserved, pronouncing its alcoholic content to be minimal. Pronouncing its algolic contender be mineral. Pronouncing my own name with difficulty. After kneeling in the toilet for some time with my head resting in the bowl I felt fighting fit again and all set to lie down. It was then that I found my wallet missing and did my best to spoil Waldo's celebration by telling him that one of his guests must have lifted it from my jacket. It was courteous of him to arrange a lift home for me instead of throwing me in the canal. When I sobered up a couple of days later it became evident that the wallet must have first of all dropped through the large hole which had developed in the bottom of my jacket's inner pocket and then fallen through the detached lining into the street before I even got to the party. It was still a good jacket otherwise though, with leather buttons like scout woggles.

So the week at the OVC hostel was all used up. One of my cabin mates, the one who had stood to attention in front of Buckingham Palace, moved out to fulfil his ambition of becoming a British officer who would protrude from the top of a rapidly moving armoured car while wearing a beret. At Sydney University he had been an actor but it was now clear that this training had always had no other purpose except to further the attainment of his real aim in life. Though his hyphenated surname would probably have got him the job anyway, it couldn't have hurt his chances that he wore clothes like Dennis Price and talked like Terry-Thomas. I had little patience with his hunger for military tradition but hated to see him go. My other cabin mate was in London to study music. Having made his arrangements, he now moved off and started doing so. Talking grandly of my intention to take a small flat in Knightsbridge, I managed to get some loose change off him before he left, but not enough, and since he was the very man I had touched in order to finance the Singapore suit I could scarcely dun him for a more substantial contribution. A postal order from home would be another week arriving. The snow in Hyde Park was not deep enough for me to build an igloo and my suitcase, although absurdly large when carried, was too cramped to live in. So I lugged it around another corner and occupied the living-room floor of two girls from Sydney's North Shore who had known me at university. After a year in London they were still in Earls Court. I was in no position to mock their lack of enterprise. They were well brought up, well spoken, well equipped and well organised – too well organised to put up with a permanent hobo camp on their parlour carpet. Curmudgeonly, this reluctance, because each evening after helping to drink their wine I generously offered to sleep with either or both. But they shared their meals with me, stuffed my shoes with paper before drying them in the stove, advised me on the purchase of a blue duffle-coat, and helped me look for somewhere to live.

Gently they discouraged my notions of seeking a maisonette in Bayswater or a mews house in Belgravia. There was a bed and breakfast boarding house in Swiss Cottage that wanted only three pounds ten shillings a week. When my postal order came, the girls very kindly drove me there. It was a long way from Kangaroo Valley and when their Volkswagen Beetle splurged away along the overlapping lines of grey slush I stood in the snow beside my mock leather suitcase and felt that I was ashore at last. My boats were burning and I was too far inland to see the flames. I resolved to grow a beard.

2

Beyond the Valley of the Kangaroos

My new home was nondescript, in the strict sense of there being nothing to describe. Wallpaper, carpets and furniture had all been chosen so as to defeat memory. About twenty people were in residence. Most of them were failed South African and Rhodesian farmers with an accent so harsh it made mine sound like Sir John Gielgud's. You met them not only at breakfast but in the evening as well, all sitting together watching 'Tonight' on television and shouting at the black man who sang the topical calypso. We were downstairs together because there was nothing we were allowed to do upstairs in our rooms alone. The list of rules forbade cooking in one's room, taking already cooked food to one's room, or taking food that did not need cooking to one's room. No visitors were allowed in one's room at any time for any reason: if one died, one's body would be allowed to decompose. Breathing was allowed as long as it made no noise. The same applied to sleep. Anyone who snored would wake up in the street. The proprietor had not made the mistake of retaining the original thick internal walls. They had been replaced by twice as many very thin ones, through which he and his lipless wife could accurately hear, and, some lodgers whisperingly warned me, see.

The danger of noisy sleep, however, was largely obviated by the difficulty of sleeping at all. One blanket too few had been carefully provided, and the central heating, although it visibly existed, was cold to the touch and had to be topped up by a two-bar radiator which failed to glow the first time I switched it on. When I nervously complained about this it was pointed out to me that the radiator was on a meter. Having never seen a meter before, I had thought that the grey machine squatting heavily in the corner was part of the house's electrical system. In a way it was, but making it function was up to me. I put in a shilling and the radiator came on. Gratefully I took off my top layer of T-shirts and running shorts, preparing for bed. The radiator went off. When I put in a florin the radiator glowed and fizzed for a bit longer but what the meter really liked was an enormous half-crown piece, a beautiful coin whose aesthetic appeal was enhanced by its then considerable purchasing power. I hated to see it go, and felt even worse, an hour or so later, when the meter, by instructing the radiator to dim out, signalled that it would like another coin the same size. The whole idea of paying to keep warm would have struck me as ludicrous if I could have stopped shivering. My teeth chattering like castanets, I doubled the thin pillow over my head to muffle the noise, so that it must have seemed, to my landlady poised outside in the corridor, as if I had ceased rehearsing for the title role in *Carmen* and started pain-training a rattlesnake.

My plan had been to take a low-paying menial job during the day and compose poetic masterpieces at night. After due reflection I decided that it would be preferable, at least initially, to take a high-paying job in journalism and sacrifice a small proportion of the masterpieces to expediency. From the editor of the *Sydney Morning Herald*, Angus Maude, I had a letter of introduction to one of the *Herald*'s previous editors, John Douglas Pringle, like Maude an Englishman but unlike him now back in London and editing the *Observer*, a newspaper whose every issue I had devoured in Australia six weeks late, and which I was now able, with admiration increased still further by understanding, to read on the day of publication. I had vowed never to use this letter of introduction, which Maude had pressed on me against my declarations of artistic purity. Crammed randomly among the socks in my giant suitcase, it had become rumpled, but a glass ashtray heated at the radiator soon ironed it relatively smooth. Cleaning up the scorched ashtray with my toothbrush took somewhat longer. Armed with the letter and with a tartan tie thoughtfully added to the Hawaiian shirt, I went to see Pringle at the *Observer*'s building in Blackfriars. Eyeing my incipient beard with what I took to be grudging appreciation of its bohemian *élan*, he asked me what languages I could read and I said English. He asked me what I wanted to do and I said write features. As I ashed my duty-free Rothmans filter on to his carpet, he pointed out that he already had a building full of young feature writers who could read at least one foreign language, wrote perfectly acceptable English and had the additional virtue of knowing quite a lot about Britain, since they had been brought up in that country, i.e. this country. My ejection from his office followed so shortly upon my entrance into it that the two events were effectively continuous. What made it more galling was that I could see his point. There wasn't really very much I could contribute to British journalism. On the other hand there probably wasn't very much it could contribute to my artistic development, so perhaps this was less a set-back than a reprieve.

Back at what I had by now learned to call my digs, the problem of laundry loomed large. Open at the foot of my bed, the giant suitcase had nothing left in it that had not already been classified at least twice as too dirty to be worn, and some of my socks were twitching where they lay. So I bundled the whole heap into one of the landlady's threadbare pillowcases and crunched off along a pavement of newly refrozen slush to the nearest launderette, otherwise known as the coin-wash, or – inaccurately but more evocatively – the bag-wash. (Strictly speaking it was only a bag-wash if you left somebody else holding the bag, and if you stayed to tend the machine yourself it was a coin-wash, but as usually happens, the fine semantic point gave way before the attractions of sonority.) The launderette had two rows of seats down the middle, back to back, so that everyone could watch his or her machine. The place was jammed and I had to wait for both a machine and a seat. During the waiting time I read the instructions. Large coins would be required for the machine and smaller ones to obtain a cup of soap. When my turn finally came I loaded the machine with a convincing nonchalance, poured in a cup of soap and sat down between two South Africans who were smiling to themselves. I could tell they were South Africans because (a) when they talked across me it was like being beaten up, and (b) two people from any other nation would have arranged to sit beside each other if they wanted to conduct a conversation. After ten minutes of going *gwersh gwersh* my machine proffered an explanation of why my companions had been smiling, snorting and clubbing each other with verbal truncheons of crushed Dutch. The window in the front of the machine having whited out completely, the flap in the top popped open and a gusher of suds began gouting out, enveloping the machine and advancing inexorably across the floor. It was an albino volcano. The South Africans were beside themselves and I was between them. They even laughed with that accent. Finally the woman in charge of the establishment came wading through the foam and added the antidote, some form of contra-detergent which killed the suds off inside the machine. I was handed a squeegee with which to contain the gleaming cloud around it.

After the second rinse, my clothes were ready to be slopped into a plastic basket and transferred to a centrifuge which would rid them of excess water. I was interested to note, during the transfer, that my shirts had taken on some of the colour of my socks. The South Africans had noticed this too and were reaching across my temporarily empty seat to hit each other with rolled-up copies of the *News of the World*, having apparently given up hope of reducing each other to unconsciousness by voice alone. The rattle of the centrifuge drowned out their merry cries. Next came the tumble drier, which required a large coin for half an hour's tumble. It had a bigger window than the washing machine and gave you a better show, but at the end of it most of my clothes still felt wet, so I put in another coin and set them tumbling again. Resolving to bring a book next time – Prescott's *The Conquest of Mexico* in three volumes would be about the right length – I occupied myself with observing how the yellow tint of the window was making my whites look tea-coloured instead of the pale bluish-grey they had been when I put them in. When the drier at last finished its second stint I opened the window and found that all my drip-dry shirts had indeed gone slightly saffron in colour – clearly as a preliminary to catching fire, because they were so hot I could hardly touch them. There was a riot of harshly accented laughter in the background.

When I got the shirts back to what I hated to call home, they proved to be not just aureate in hue, but brittle in texture. I put one of them on and a cuff broke off. The nylon polymer had been transformed into some friable variety of perspex. Another worrying aspect was the pillowcase, which I should have washed along with its contents. I would have to sleep holding my nose. But at least my personal linen was now fragrant enough to allow me a night out with the Australians at a party in Melbury Road, on the Holland Park side of Kensington High Street. This was perilously close to Earls Court, which I had vowed never to enter again, but as an evening's distraction it beat watching television with the

Voortrekkers. The previous evening there had been a play about a black African freedom fighter earning the respect of the security police by his bravery. Whenever the weary policemen stopped hitting him there were shouts of protest from my fellow lodgers. The uproar reached a climax when the black was allowed to make his dying speech without being assaulted. 'Thet's what's *rewning* Efrica,' said a voice from a winged chintz chair, 'litting a keffir talk to them like thet.' Another chintz chair agreed. 'Thet's right,' it said. 'They mist not be allowed to answer *beck*.'

Far from sure why I had come to England at all, I was nevertheless certain that it hadn't been in order to hang out with my compatriots, but unaccountably I now craved their well-modulated tones. With a gallon tin of brown water under each arm I climbed the stairs to the top-floor flat of a house in Melbury Road which had held a large Australian expatriate contingent since the time of the Pre-Raphaelites, one of whom had rented the studio in the back yard. There were fifty duffle-coats draped over the banisters and about a hundred people frantically twisting inside the flat itself, data which suggested that each couple had arrived sharing the one coat. The girl to whom I had sworn eternal fealty was half the world away and I was feeling friendless, but this new style of dancing, in which the partners did not actually touch each other, was a heaven-sent opportunity to move in on other men's women. I had been practising the Twist in my room and because of the necessity to remain undetected by the landlady's sonar I had developed a finely calculated frictionless style, in which my feet trembled noiselessly on the spot while the rest of my body alternated between drying its back with an imaginary towel and pointing out the approach of hostile aircraft. All this was done in a closed-eyed trance, but I can't believe that I looked any more ridiculous than the rest of the men and certainly I inflicted far fewer injuries through inadvertent karate blows with the flying feet, although my rapidly and randomly extended pointing fingers were admittedly apt to make contact with somebody else's eyeball. A polite squeal resulting from just such an infringement brought me face to face with one of my erstwhile girlfriends, who had already been in London for a year, working as an editorial assistant for a publisher. Unfortunately she had embraced Catholicism in the interim, which turned out to mean that I was not allowed to embrace her. It was quite an accommodating broom cupboard that I backed her into – much larger than the sort of thing we had been used to in Sydney – but she warded off my beer-breath, bristle-chin importunities with a regretful knee and insisted on going home with the English publishing type who had brought her, some woofling galah with a Morgan.

Next evening I took her to see *Hiroshima mon amour* and we became the only couple in history ever to see that film and not get into bed together afterwards. We sat on it instead. Her bed-sitting room in Chalk Farm was cosy enough if you didn't mind the crucifixes. 'You saw nothing in Hiroshima.' You can say that again. She looked prettier than ever in all that wool. Even her tights were made of wool. It became clear that they would stay in place. But she was generous with something more substantial – practical assistance. Rupert, the goof in the Morgan, was looking for a free-lance copy editor. With my *Sydney Morning Herald* training I could do it on my head. Helping myself to more of her wine, I explained my firm intention not to compromise. But the duty-free cigarettes were running low and at this rate even my bed and breakfast would soon be too expensive. A temporary sell-out might be advisable. Having finished off her reserve bottle of banana-skin Beaujolais, I took the typescript she had given me and set off on foot through the cold, foggy night towards Swiss Cottage. Navigating by a sure Australian instinct for the lie of the land, I saw quite a lot of Maida Vale, and got home in good time to be locked out.

The typescript was for a children's book about dinosaurs. 'As massive as a modern home and weighing many tons, Man would have been dwarfed by these massive creatures . . . ' I spent the next two days sorting out tenses, expunging solecisms and re-allocating misplaced clauses to the stump from which they had been torn loose by the sort of non-writing writer for whom grammar is not even a mystery, merely an irrelevance. Short of rewriting the thing entirely, I couldn't have done the job better, so it was with confidence that I posted the doctored script, together with a covering letter stating that a mere thirty pounds a week would be about the right rate, in view of the fact that I would be working only casually, in between my own literary projects.

Hampstead Heath was a slush curry of dead leaves but lent itself readily to the creative meanderings of young writers with high expectations and cold hands stuffed into duffle-coat pockets. In the next few days I joined this ambling band, ploughing a lonely furrow to criss-cross with theirs. On a park bench padded with newspapers I sat shivering while a new kind of poem formed in my notebook. It was a poem I could understand. Until then, most of my poems had been devotedly incomprehensible. Now they were becoming comprehensible, a transformation that would have allowed me to detect their sentimentality if they had not been so true to my feelings, which were sentimental. But I was warmer than I would have been in my room, and when inspiration failed I could always make the short pilgrimage to Keats's house. It looked compact and elegant among the leafless trees – compact and elegant like him. He wrote the 'Ode to a Nightingale' there, but although I was mad about his odes at that time, the ode I was maddest about was the one on Melancholy. *Sudden from heaven like a weeping cloud.* I thought of that line when I was walking down Frognal and the rain caught me with nowhere to hide. So I got back home soaked, just in time for the evening post, which informed me that I hadn't got the editorial job. Apparently what I had written in my covering note – that the thing needed rewriting entirely – was what I should have done. So once again I had been saved from selling out. Drying myself in front of the radiator while the meter ate half-crowns like Smarties, I tried to feel relieved, but it was getting less easy all the time.

3

Soul for Sale

Never, I had vowed, would I sell my soul to an advertising agency. Not even if I was starving. Not even if I had no ceiling over my head. Yet starvation was only one step down from the breakfast I was getting every morning, and the ceiling over my head had South Africans on the other side using it as a floor. Waldo invited me to a party he was throwing for all his flash new friends in English advertising. I went along in order to be disgusted by their materialist values. There were plenty of materialist values on display, starting with the traffic jam of early production model E-type Jaguars parked out in the street. The men were reasonably easy to sneer at, with their elastic-sided, chisel-toed Chelsea boots and girlish length of hair. As usually happens in such circumstances, the real challenge was presented by the women. One of them was called Brenda and she was so glossily pretty that it was hatred at first sight. Unfortunately she was clever and funny too, so it was not easy to remain hostile. She was married to some pipe-sucking Nigel who tried to interest me in how David Ogilvy had once told him that if you fouled the air in somebody's bathroom, all you had to do was strike a match and the atmosphere would instantly return to its pristine sweetness, even if the bathroom were as big as an aircraft hangar. I can remember this with such clarity only because I was in the process of falling in love with his wife at the time. But she was married, and would have been even more frightening if single. It was clear just from what she had on her that it took a lot of money to run such a woman. The time had come for a modification of values. Faust was ready to negotiate. Casting Waldo as Mephistopheles, I drew him aside and asked him how to set about becoming a copy-writer. Since he had had to endure my callow jibes against his profession many times in the past, it was big of him to answer this question with useful information instead of the horse laugh. Apparently there was a vacancy coming up at Simpson, Sampson, Ranulph and Rolfe. He would get me through the door and from then on it would be up to me.

Reassured, I danced a few times with Brenda and tried not to be disappointed when she had to leave early with a gouged eye. She and Nigel climbed into a ludicrously small new car calling itself a Mini. With my bump for technology I could tell straight away that such a glorified toy would never catch on, but still I couldn't imagine anything more desirable than being in a very small car with a girl like Brenda. All it would take would be a few scintillating jingles, and vroom-vroom. 'You'll *piss* it in,' said Waldo. 'Just remember to cover your mouth when you belch and don't stub your fags out on the Axminster.'

Waldo was as good as his word and I had barely a day to prepare my spontaneous utterances before reporting to St James's Square and being ushered into the suave presence of SSRR's senior partner and creative chief, the legendary P.H.S. 'Plum' Rolfe. He had Hush Puppies on his feet and a tweed tie around his neck, but the tie was loose and his feet were on his desk, so it was possible to relax – something I would not otherwise have found easy to do, because I was a bit worried about my wardrobe. The suit from Singapore had still not arrived and by now I had begun to wonder if the green sports coat and the wrecked shoes were quite the thing, especially as my scorched drip-dry shirts tended to shatter no matter how carefully I buttoned them up, making my façade look like a vandalised housing development unless I not only arranged the tartan tie to cover the damage but contrived to keep it that way while lounging casually in a chair. But Rolfe seemed to like my poems. While he was opening my old Sydney University magazines to the places marked, I tried a few rehearsed spontaneous utterances and he liked them too. It was even more encouraging when he turned out to like the unrehearsed ones still better. He told me to send him a five thousand word essay on why I wanted to be an advertising man and then come back again in a fortnight.

Having written the essay that same evening, I went next morning to the Mayfair branch of the Bank of NSW and raised a £50 overdraft on the strength of being a hot job prospect for a top agency. Since I had no account at the bank and was clearly opening one only in order to see the assistant manager and touch him for a loan, it will be appreciated that my powers of persuasion were benefiting from a surge of confidence. No doubt the beard helped. Looking less like an oversight by now and more like an act of defiance, it must have presented an over-whelming challenge to the assistant manager's bourgeois inhibitions. I should have asked him for a hundred.

A small part of the ensuing desert of vast eternity I was able to spend marching from Aldermaston with Waldo's advertising contingent. Actually we didn't march from Aldermaston. Like 90 per cent of the march-ers we marched from just outside London, but it was called marching from Aldermaston and felt wonderful. That was the whole point, I need hardly say: feeling wonderful. The whole thing was essentially a religious festival. It wasn't politics, it was performance. I was aware of this even at the time, since my radical socialism, which in my own eyes made me an implacable outsider like Bakunin, necessarily included a deep hostility to

37

the Soviet Union, which I already knew, long before Solzhenitsyn's revelations, to have been a murder factory on a scale barely hinted at by Khrushchev's speech to the 20th Party Congress in 1956. No amount of stupidity on America's part could allay the uncomfortable feeling that unilateral nuclear disarmament had no more in common with multilateral nuclear disarmament than insanity had in common with sanity. But solidarity between opposites being possible for as long as it remains ineffective, the party got bigger and louder while you watched. I danced along with the Ban-the-Bombers because they were the nicest people. I even sang with them, which was the ultimate tribute to their sweetness, because those songs were terrible. 'Ban the Bomb, it's now or never / Ban the Bomb, for ev-er more!' Actually I just moved my lips. Like a Shadow Cabinet Minister pretending to sing 'The Red Flag' at a Labour Party Conference, I was too bashful to pronounce the words. But I was there, acting out a fantasy because it was more fun than what I knew to be truth. Brenda was there too, of course, and the chance to stride along beside her would have taken me on a pilgrimage to Lhasa if necessary. It turned out she had all the same doubts as I had but was there because of Nigel, who was there because everybody else was. If the Sixties ever had a real beginning, an emblematic event that set the tone for an epoch, that was it – thousands upon thousands of nice people all behaving as if the irritable shrugging off of awkward facts was a kind of dance. Indeed just such a dance soon came in on the heels of the Twist, and was called the Shake.

Flushed with virtue, I turned up in St James's Square on the appointed day with my shirt cuffs protruding just the correct inch from the sleeves of my green jacket, an adjustment made easier by the fact that they had parted company from the actual shirt. The Singapore suit, had it arrived in time, would undoubtedly have been an advantage, but once again Mr Rolfe looked reassuringly bohemian, smoking no hands while he leafed through my essay. He had never read a more convincing case, he said, for how primal creativity could be combined with a job in advertising. He had no doubt that I could write Australia's answer to *Paradise Lost* in the evenings while concurrently promoting cornflakes all day. What he and Messrs Simpson, Sampson and Ranulph were after, however, was someone who wanted to do nothing else except promote the cornflakes. They wanted someone for whom the poetry was not separate from the cornflakes, but actually *in* the cornflakes and *of* the cornflakes. Like Frosties, I suggested: the sugar wasn't separate from the cornflakes, it was in them and of them. Rolfe said I had hit it exactly, but didn't give me any extra points for the insight. 'Face it,' he said, smiling without dropping the cigarette, 'you aren't modest enough to be corruptible. Getting rich isn't what you're really after. You'd always be writing something for yourself on our time.' He had the great gift of making you feel that you had been turned down because you were too good, so I didn't start feeling miserable until I was outside in the square, where I had a hallucination, startling in its clarity, of Brenda retreating into the distance while waving to me from the passenger seat of a speeding Maserati. The pavements, though cold to my perforated shoes, were dry for once, so I walked all the way home to Swiss Cottage, feeling more ill, broke and woebegone all the time. The Singapore suit was waiting for me when I got there. It had been forwarded from the OVC and was wrapped in thick brown paper through which several peep-holes had been torn, presumably by customs officers. The conviction nagged me that if I had been wearing it I would have got the job. At least it would ensure that I got the next job.

Unwrapped, the Singapore suit was impressive for its weight of cloth. When I put it on and stood in front of the sliver of glass which the landlady evidently supposed to constitute a full-length mirror, I looked the image of

39

bespoke respectability. You had to hand it to those oriental tailors. They might be flatterers – 'What muscular forearms,' they had whispered as they plied the tape measure, 'what powerful thighs' – but they knew how to cut cloth. Then I lifted my arms to adjust the mirror, and discovered that I couldn't see. The shoulders of the jacket had immediately risen to engulf my head. When I put my arms back down, vision returned. Perhaps I had just moved too suddenly. Tentatively I lifted my right arm. The right shoulder of the jacket went up past my ear. Ditto for the left side. Even more slowly I lifted both arms. Blackout. There was no spare cloth in the armpits: the gussets, or whatever they were called, were missing. Presumably it was the Singapore style of suit, designed for a subtle oriental people not much given to gesture. Anyway, if I kept my hands by my sides it looked quite good.

4

Into the Hinterland

There was enough left of my overdraft to finance a change of residence. My Swiss Cottage landlady, clearly not charmed by the misshapen ashtray or whatever had happened to her pillowcase, had raised the rent, perhaps also because the end of winter was in the air, with a congruent diminution of revenue from the electricity meter. It was time to rent my first bed-sitting room. In those days a bed-sit all to yourself could be had for three pounds a week, a significant amount less than I was paying at Swiss Cottage. As I compose this sentence, it costs about thirty pounds a week in London to share a two-room flat with three other people and each of them wants to interview you personally before okaying you for the short list, after which the final selection is by written examination. Even allowing for the way money has declined from twenty times its current value in as many years, lonely life was more possible then. Nowadays the young and broke are lucky to sleep on the pavements, while the unlucky ones get chatted up in a pub by a kind-looking chap, taken home to his place, strangled, cut up into small pieces and flushed down a drain. Comparatively little of that was going on in my time. John Christie had merely killed the sort of older people that nobody would miss. The sort of younger people that nobody would miss were not yet on the scene.

Pretty well the worst that could happen to you was to answer the wrong advertisement, which I duly did, ending up in a first-floor horror of a room at the high end of Tufnell Park Road. The other side of the Heath was not necessarily the other side of the world. Kentish Town was only just up the hill and already showing signs of gentrification. But gentrification hadn't touched my room. Putrefaction, yes. Trying to guess what colour the wallpaper had been before the attack by the brown virus from beyond the planets, I vowed that my stay in the Tufnell Park area would be a short one. Somehow, if necessary by a temporary submission to capitalist values, my fortunes would be transformed, after which it would be a small flat in Knightsbridge with easy access to Harrods food hall.

Or perhaps a large flat in Chelsea. At about this time I presumed on my slight acquaintance with Joyce Grenfell to get myself invited around to Elm Park Gardens for a much needed proper lunch, involving such luxuries, long missing from my diet, as beans, lettuce and other foodstuffs coloured green. It was our second meeting. I had first met her when I was a member of the Sydney University Journalists' Club and she had come to Australia on a theatrical tour. We had sent her a luncheon invitation which she threw us into a panic by accepting. Since then I had written her a barrage of tiresomely clever letters which she had been kind enough to answer – probably, I am now able to see, as a means of doing penance, because her nature was so saintly that she looked on duty as a blessing. Semi-bearded and weirdly clad, I sat there in the otherwise immaculate kitchen of her flat, explaining revolutionary socialism while consuming her food. She asked me if there was anything I needed. What I needed was an independent income in five figures, but to my credit – there was so little to my credit that I feel justified in the boast – I didn't put the bite on her. Instead I informed her that

42

everything was going according to plan. I had shaken myself free of materialist values and the results were already showing in my poetry. Some recent examples of this I read to her unasked. She countered by trying out one of her new sketches on me. It was the one about the old lady who posts the dead rabbit through the car window. I laughed helplessly, but while walking home suffered from bitter afterthoughts. Her work was so obviously the finished product, whereas everything of my own, though it struck me as masterly in the hour of its composition, seemed fragmentary only a few days later. The contrast was made doubly galling by my secret agreement with Ken Tynan's published opinion that the Grenfell school of revue was irredeemably genteel and therefore belonged in the dustbin of history, along with the plays of Terence Rattigan and of almost everybody else except Brecht. You could tell that she was a historical back-number by the way she lived, with all those carpets and cushions and a portrait of her mother by Sargent up on the Regency-striped wall. There was even a woman to wait on table. Comfort and good manners stood revealed as an expression of privilege, and the fact that the privilege had all been worked for just went to show.

None of that back in Tufnell Park, at the cutting edge of the bohemian experience. Though spring was on its way, there were still enough cold nights left to demonstrate what was involved in the change from electricity to gas. Over the basin – an early Sung dynasty ceramic artefact which had been pieced back together by a blind archaeologist – there was an early-model Ascot gas water-heater with several levers which had to be swivelled in the right order when the thing was ignited. If the correct procedure was observed, the machine merely exploded. But if you got it wrong you could be in serious trouble. Even the radiator, or fire, ran on gas. It consisted of a single lattice-work pipe-clay heating element standing vertically in the cusp of a metal reflector, which would have thrown the heat forward had it still been shiny, but which was now, and obviously had been for a long time, black enough to absorb any bold calorie that might threaten to escape from the barely pink glow of the clapped-out element operating at full throttle. For cooking, there was not only the mandatory free-standing gas ring but a proper stove, this latter item having been billed as a luxury extra which could well have warranted the bed-sit being advertised as a flat with kitchenette.

The first hour of the first night revealed that all the bedclothes provided were insufficient to keep my feet warm. Lying there fully dressed with the blankets bound tightly around my feet and knotted, I reluctantly calculated that the gas fire would have to be left running as well. With my feet still bound I hopped over to the gas meter, inserted half a crown, lit the fire, hopped back to bed and lay down. After twenty minutes the element had done little more than assume the colour of a raspberry ice lolly, so I hopped over to the stove, lit that too, left the door open so that the heat would pervade the room, hopped back to bed again, and was just manoeuvring myself into the horizontal position when the fire and the stove both gave a mutter, sputter and guttural pop. It was a total flame-out. The Swiss Cottage electricity meter had been merely a gourmet. The Tufnell Park gas meter was a gourmand. It was Moloch. Obviously it melted the cash payments down for their constituent bullion and gave no more gas than was in the coins themselves.

Winter was almost over but abject poverty was clearly only just beginning. My book-buying habits were no help. From Australia I had brought only one book with me: *Studies in Empirical Philosophy* by John Anderson. The scrupulous realism of Anderson had been either a direct influence on, or a cause of reaction in, almost every Sydney University student of recent years except me. Typically I had failed to avail myself of his instruction while he was still giving it out free every day in the form of lectures. But on board ship, with the man himself safely dead, buried and falling ever further behind, I had submitted myself at last to his magnetic force. Though I was to be a long time making myself proof against the urge to escape from reality into righteous anger, and am perhaps not entirely immune from its blandishments yet, the example of Anderson's critical scepticism struck deep. 'It will be a sign of renewed progress, then,' wrote Anderson in his devastating critique of Marxism's philosophical pretensions, 'when we see revolutionists divesting themselves of the idealistic elements in their philosophy and embracing a consistent realism. Meanwhile, it is the philosopher's business to be realistic, to attack idealism wherever he finds it, to consider constantly what is the case.' Anderson's was the voice of reason. But the voice of poetry had not lost its power to intoxicate, especially as embodied in the works of Shakespeare, whom I now rediscovered with a fervour explicable only in terms of my new geographical proximity to his old stamping grounds. True, Tufnell Park had not been the location of any of his several theatres. Indeed if you were to construct a map showing all those purlieus of London even tenuously relevant to Shakespeare's life, there would be a large blank area of which Tufnell Park would be the centre. Not even in the rarely performed *Henry III Part 4* does anyone say 'Brave friends await full-armed at Tufnell Park.' Nevertheless I heard the whispered echo of his light tread everywhere, and when, in a Charing Cross Road second-hand bookshop, I found a set of the four-volume Nonesuch Shakespeare in the small format, the consideration that it cost exactly as much money as I had in the world was outweighed by the sensuous allure of the gold-stamped buckram half-bindings, marbled boards and opaque paper. Although it rated nowhere as a scholarly text, the set when stood upright on my rickety linoleum-topped bedside table helped to make my cell look intentional in its austerity, as if it belonged to St

Jerome rather than Caryl Chessman. The effect was further enhanced by the purchase of Louis MacNeice's personal copy of *Practical Criticism*, by I. A. Richards, which I found spine-upright on a trestle table outside the bay window of a small bookshop in Bloomsbury. On the end-paper was the price in pencil, half a crown, and MacNeice's signature in faded ink. Perhaps the bookshop owner could not read. I bought the book for its resonance as an association copy and added it to my table-top library.

Even when bought as bargains, this library's constituent volumes were costing me money I didn't have. To compound the felony, the very books which were eventually to teach me a measure of humility had at first the effect of encouraging me in the opposite, so that I pursued the life of the mind as if the world owed me a living. If the mind develops at all in such circumstances, it is likely to do so leaving certain gaps, one of which will be the failure to realise that to borrow money without the intention of paying it back is a form of theft. I, on the other hand, believed that property was theft – a more glamorous idea altogether, and one which encouraged the notion that if you could induce an acquaintance to give you some of his property in the form of money you were practically a policeman. Luckily I was circumscribed in my begging from friends, first of all by a shortage of friends and then by their own shortage of cash. Sources of small-scale loans with which to pay back large-scale loans were drying up. But I was determined to live the artistic life, and there were quite a few extremely artistic activities which could be pursued at no expense, if you were prepared to walk there instead of ride. Every time the National Gallery held the British people to ransom by announcing that a Leonardo cartoon would go to America unless they stumped up, I would walk to the gallery, study the great drawing on display, and generously insert into the collection box some small-denomination aluminium coin from Singapore or Port Said. If the White-chapel Gallery held a Barbara Hepworth retrospective I would trek down the Holloway Road to the East End and spend hours caressing her brass volumes and bronze volutes with a famished eye. The famished stomach I placated with fish and chips bought from a glorified roadside whelk-stall just near the gallery. The stall featured a lot of other weird stuff along with the whelks, including what looked like cross-sectional research samples of a prehistoric worm colony trapped in a glaciated bog. These, I was told, were jellied eels. While I was being told this, a small bow-legged man in a flat cap came shambling up, purchased some of the jellied eels, and began, with quivering, palsied hands, to cram them into his asymmetrical maw. He assured me, between noisy mouthfuls, that a life-long diet of jellied eels had made him what he was.

Kenwood House was another free treat, not just for the pictures but for the Adam interiors. I began to have an eye for the clean sweep and jocund formality of the plaster ceiling in a grand English house, perhaps impelled by the contrast it presented to my ceiling in Tufnell Park, which looked as if a loosely stretched and seriously crumpled old tarpaulin had been stuccoed with night-soil. Whether Kenwood House had an eye for me was another question. Certainly my appearance would have startled the original owner if he had still been around to greet his guests. Winter by now was transforming itself into spring by way of a transitional period consisting mainly of mud. The air, if not exactly balmy, was too warm for a duffle-coat, so I was wearing my new combat jacket, bought from one of the many army-surplus stores along Holloway Road which were still occupied with distributing the excess production stimulated by the Korean war. This combat jacket was not the American quilted kind which actually kept you warm. It was more the British kind whose chief function was to get dirty. But clad in it

I could imagine myself looking interesting and dangerous; not a man to be messed with. Anyone taking due note of my now more-than-half-formed beard might have decided that I was a man who could be depended upon to mess with himself, but to distract the world's attention from my head there was what was going on around my feet. These were enveloped in a pair of shoes given to me by Joyce Grenfell. She said that they had been given to her husband but that they had not fitted. She was a woman who never lied in her life. In this one case there might have been an element of diplomatic inexactitude. I suspect that they had fitted, but that he had rejected them for another reason. With thick uppers and an invulnerable three-ply sole, they were well made – far and away the highest quality footwear that I would enjoy for many years to come – but they were tanned a colour so reddish it was almost strawberry. It was another episode in my long history of unsuitable shoes, a story which is not yet closed and would need a book of its own. Let's just say that even now, when I have learned to dress as plainly as possible, I still get so impatient with the whole time-consuming business of covering up exposed skin that I will buy the first thing that catches my eye, and that when it comes to shoes the first thing that catches your eye is the last thing you should ever put on your feet. It is almost better to be an impulse shirt-buyer than an impulse shoe-buyer. I have worn shirts that made people think I was a retired Mafia hit-man or a Yugoslavian sports convenor from Split, but I have worn shoes that made people think I was insane.

Anyway, when I turned up for my next attempt to land a job, that was how I looked – like Judas Iscariot deserting across the 38th Parallel in shoes stolen from a clown. A wine merchant called T. H. Lawrence (I remember it wasn't D. E. Lawrence but was something equally unlikely, so it must have been T. H. Lawrence) placed a classified advertisement for a young man to learn the wine trade. Required qualifications would be a degree in the humanities, physical strength, and an interest in fine wines. The first qualification I certainly had. The second I still had in part, despite the effects of eating fat-fried food every night in a dark room. The third was more of a problem. At the time I left Australia it was already on the verge of becoming one of the great wine countries of the world, but I won't pretend that I was in any way *au courant* with the incipient viticultural breakthrough. My idea of a fine wine was one that merely stained your teeth without stripping off the enamel. In Britain I had discovered Woodpecker cider and resorted to wine only when it was on offer free at Melbury Road parties, where it usually issued from a large green bottle marked with the name of the Hungarian composer Janos Riesling. Nevertheless I had picked up a certain amount of technical chat and reckoned I could get away with a short interview if I kept it laconic. Since the address was that of a country pub in Kent, I eschewed the Singapore suit. Also the red shoes were the only ones I currently possessed. To wear them in combination with the Singapore suit would be to set up a contrast in colour which even I could see was a blow to the optic nerve. If I kept my arms to my sides, the dark cloth of the Singapore suit lulled the viewer's eyes as they travelled down my person, which only made the dissonance more stunning when it was revealed that I was standing in two bidets full of strawberry soda. The combat jacket made for a more meant-looking ensemble, in my opinion. This opinion could have been mistaken but I doubt that it would have made any difference if I had arrived suitably attired for an investiture. When I finally fetched up at T. H. Lawrence's rustic hostelry after long, lost detours up and down winding hedge-lined single carriageways, the proprietor came to the door, took one look at me and quite obviously loathed what he saw happening on the lower part of my face.

'Oh dear,' he snapped. 'Beard.' Generously I stood nonplussed, instead of retaliating, which I could have done by pointing out how hard his blue blazer and handlebar moustache were trying to make me think of the Battle of Britain, an effect undone by his extreme brevity of stature. He might very well have flown against the Germans, but only on the back of a pigeon. I either managed to bite all this back or else never thought of it, probably the latter. Scott Fitzgerald's Nick Carraway says at some point that any demonstration of complete self-confidence draws a stunned tribute from him. Even today, when some oaf who has confused rudeness with blunt speech tells me exactly what he thinks, I tend to stand there wondering what I have done to deserve it, instead of telling him exactly what I think right back. In those days I was even more easily wrong-footed, not having begun to realise that the boor has a built-in advantage which can be countered on the spot only at the cost of becoming a boor oneself. I used to worry about having no quick answer, and was thus bereft of self-esteem as well as of speech. So when T. H. Lawrence asked me what I thought of the recent French and German vintages I was not best placed to give a convincing summary. My mumbled generalisations got me as far as the bar, but there he poured a glass of yellowish white wine and asked me to taste it.

'This is a 1960 Trockenbocken hock from Schlocken-glocken,' he rapped, or words to that effect. 'Selling it through my club for a quid a bottle. What do you think?' I sniffed it, said it had a nice nose, sipped it, said it had a nice bottom, and sank the rest of it in one. 'You know bugger all about wines,' announced T. H. Lawrence matter-of-factly, in the clipped tones of a veteran Spitfire pilot telling the duty officer that the new boy on the squadron had made an unauthorised solo pass over Rhine-Hopstein airfield at nought feet, copped a packet of light flak, and flown straight into a petrol tanker.

'Wasted your time coming down here. Wasted mine too. Cut my hedges for lunch and we'll call it square.'

Starting either side of the pub's gravelled forecourt, hedgerow stretched in each direction along the roadside for as far as the eye could see. With the clippers provided, I went at it and in less than an hour had trimmed a surprising amount of hedge – something like one and a half square yards. T. H. Lawrence the wee Wing Commander didn't help by periodically emerging from his ops room to laugh good-naturedly at my efforts and confess his wonder that an Ossie (*sic*) should be so inept at the kind of activity which must be fairly standard in the Backout or Backthere or whatever it was called, har har. Like many Englishmen of his class and IQ, the Sanforised Squadron Leader was either incapable of pronouncing the word Aussie correctly – i.e., with a 'z' sound instead of an 's' – or else did not want to, for fear of spoiling the priceless joke whose other elements included the Outback, kangaroos, and the hilarious fantasy of people walking around upside-down. 'I expect you Ossies see plenty of kangaroos in the Backout when you're walking along upside-down' was a standard line, invariably preluded, postluded and punctuated by self-applauding shouts of laughter from a large mouth held six inches from my face. T. H. Lawrence's version of the same theme differed only in that his mouth was held six inches from my chest. Stripped to the waist and seething with misdirected fury, I clipped like a maniac and got the whole hedge trimmed in time for a late lunch.

My lunch was served on a trestle table in the open air. A piece of stiff white cheese smeared with yellow pickle had been clamped in a vise of partly refreshened bread. There was also half a pint of brown water. These victuals were brought to me with a practised display of weary magnanimity by the abbreviated Air Commodore himself. I had been hungry and thirsty until I saw these things. But the sun was almost warm and there was the additional pleasure of watching the farmers arrive for their midday break. It was a highly traditional sight. You got the sense that it had been going on for a millennium. From Lagondas, Graber-bodied Alvis Grey Ladies and V-8 Aston Martins they emerged barking in tweeds. 'Nigola!' they yelled. 'Over heah, Nigola! I say Nigola! Over *heah*!' Yet their wives and mistresses made me want to keep my eyes open, even if my fingers were in my ears. Merely quacking while their menfolk bayed like hounds, they looked all the more desirable for their daunting self-assurance. In London I had seen nothing like them. Perhaps it was the district. More probably it was spring. Sitting out there with those wonderful, hand-woven, gentleman's-relish women under the same sun, I was made invisible by my appearance, like a satyr in an old engraving who blends with a gnarled tree-trunk and its attendant shrubbery. Thus I could catch the perfume of their corduroy and cashmere as they yelped to each other about banging along to Harvey Nichols for a spree. Lust and envy made their usual explosive mixture in my soul. If one of those long-striding creatures had smiled at me I would have thrown back my head and given the warrior-call of the bull ape. But nobody infringed my frustrated privacy except the miniature Marshal of Air Vice, Group Captain T. H. 'Taffy' Lawrence, Distinguished Self-Service Restaurant and Bar.

'Finished? Good. There's a path around the back. Show you.' I thought he was showing me a quick way to the railway station, but it turned out that he was showing me the back boundary of his property, another hedge almost as long as the one in front. I could have done a bunk the minute he left me alone. Defiant, defeated anger required that I stay and make a job of it. By the time I had finished, the afternoon was almost spent, but the countryside was still a pretty sight as I walked back along the winding single-lane road to the station, occasionally leaning back sourly into the hedge while fast cars full of contented, well-dressed, well-fed people treated the road as if they owned it. Which, of course, they did.

5

Cracking the Secret Code

Just when you think things are as bad as they can get, suddenly they get worse. Not that there was a shortage of jobs. Though the reader of today might find it difficult to believe, twenty years ago in London there was casual white-collar work to burn. I, however, seemed incapable of getting in amongst it. By now I had my name down with the Professional and Executive register and it was amazing how many interviews they sent me off to that I mucked up by talking too much, talking too little or talking just the right amount but to the wrong person. I merely throw in this observation for the benefit of any younger reader, or for that matter any older reader, who has never got a job after an interview. Neither have I. An interview is where you sell yourself, and some of us are just bad salesmen, with no gift for correctly assessing the demand before we start matching it with a supply. If a clerk's job was on offer, I came on strong, filling the air with abstruse literary references, when the only references the interviewer wanted were from some previous employer saying that I had performed clerical duties to his satisfaction and not stolen the clock. If the vacancy was for an editorial assistant, on the other hand, I underplayed it, saying little and looking tough, like a one-time boundary rider who, despite the circumstances of cultivated leisure implied by his now possessing a suit made in Singapore, could still mend a fence or trap a frilled lizard. It was a disaster either way, but the second method at least had the virtue of rendering the interviewer visible at all times. Employing the first method, I had always to hold the cuffs of the Singapore suit's sleeves in a surreptitiously clenched fist while making an expansive, genius-betokening gesture, otherwise the man I was talking to would disappear as if by magic. Not long afterwards I would disappear myself, but there was nothing magic about that.

Back on the street, spring was well established and the girls of London were prettier than they had ever been or would ever be again. They were saying goodbye to the old austerity without having quite yet said the full, mad hello to Sixties fashions at their most demented. Skirts were on their way up the thigh but had not yet reached the waist. Hair was back-combed but had not yet attained the shape and consistency of a lacquered crash-helmet. Stiletto heels were long and sharp but not yet like needles, so that if a girl trod on your foot you were able to hop about in pain instead of being pinned screaming to the dance-floor. There was a new exuberance abroad, atomised libido was misty in the air, and I was out of it. No money, no prospects. Just debts, purple gums and a pair of shoes that lit up in the dark like dachshunds with scarlet fever.

But there were too many casual jobs on offer for me to go on missing out, even with my talent for being the man off the spot. Just when the only funds remaining were half a dozen Woodpecker cider bottles worth threepence each for the returned deposit, a classified advertisement led me to a London University annexe in Bloomsbury where questionnaires were being coded. A dozen casual coders were required, degree essential and qualifications in psychology desirable. Having majored in psychology at Sydney University, I was taken on as the dozenth coder. Fifteen minutes later and I would have dipped

55

out. This I could be sure of, because, fourteen minutes after I signed on, a candidate turned up who looked as mathematically gifted as Max Planck, an impression not dissipated by the slide-rule sticking out of his pocket. It was a nice change to stand there and see him turned away, instead of being turned away myself. The man in charge, a handsome young tweed-jacketed Rhodesian called Robin Jackson if it wasn't Jack Robinson, showed signs of regretting how things had transpired, but quixotically decided to stick by the arrangement already made. Banzai. I was in, at the lavish emolument, for the six weeks the job would last, of ten pounds a week before stoppages. What stoppages were I had no idea, and for the moment was too busy to ask.

The completed questionnaires contained the answers of thousands of people to hundreds of questions. These questions ranged from concrete enquiries about age and gender to a whole last page of abstract stuff about attitudes and values, whether liberal or otherwise. As I now remember it, which is vaguely, a statistically random sample of students was being assessed for demography, motivation, goals, height above sea level, etc. No doubt I was pretty hazy about it all even at the time. The typical respondent started off by saying he was a 19-year-old male and ended up rating the possibility of God's existence on a scale from one to five. In other words it was a snare for Snarks, a sieve to measure water, a machine to count sand. But to convert the written answers into a given range of symbols was a mechanical matter for anyone who had ever spent a couple of years fooling around with Personality Profiles, Thematic Apperception Tests and that old standby of university psychology departments world wide, the Minnesota Multiphasic.

We all sat around a large, polished mahogany table with Robin handing out new sheaves of uncoded questionnaires and stacking the ones we had finished into a heap. After the first hour I was on automatic pilot and using up some of the spare energy by inspecting my fellow workers as they toiled. Half of them, I was pleased to note, were females. One of these, sitting at the end of the table to my left, was a very elegant young Indian woman in a gold-trimmed sari the colour of bleached pomegranate. Her name, too sonorous to be forgotten however long I live, was Saraj. Perhaps my heart would have gone out to her if Millicent had not been sitting directly opposite me. But Millicent would probably have had the same effect if she had been sitting upstairs. She radiated so much sensuality that I could still see her after I had closed my eyes.

This is neither the time nor the place to give my conclusions about the physics and metaphysics of sexual attraction. For one thing, it would take a separate volume. For another, I doubt if anything I had to say would be of sufficient originality to warrant the effort, not to mention the trouble. Most inhibiting of all, I seriously wonder if I have yet reached any conclusions, or ever will before I die. When I do die, and come to that check-point inside the gates of Hell where the horrible Minos circles himself with his tail as an indication of the infernal level to which the new entrant is assigned, it will be no secret between me and him that during my time on Earth I suffered from – or enjoyed, if that is the preferred formula – inordinate susceptibility to female beauty. It will be the second thing that he asks me about. His first question will not demand an answer. 'Hello there, cobber! Must be a relief to be walking the right way up with no kangaroos around out there in the back! Brought your tube of Foster's? Har har.' But the next question will be harder to dodge.

I suppose it was a case of arrested development. From childhood onwards I had seen beauty in women as a revelation of universal truth, and now, in what should have been adulthood, I still did, which meant that adulthood felt like childhood, with childish behaviour as an inevitable consequence. There is a lot to be said for

57

idealising those we adore, but not if it means neglecting to listen to what they have to say. A good-looking woman, as well as being the incarnation of a Platonic concept, is quite often a human being as well. One of the cockney photographers who were at that time just beginning their rise to fame recently told me that his success with some of the world's most gorgeous women was almost entirely due to patting them on the bottom – or, as he put it, patinum honour bum. Having looked like goddesses all their lives, they had never met a man who patted them on the bottom, although they had met hundreds of men who wrote poems in their honour. Sitting at home beside my suitcase in Tufnell Park I wrote many a poem about Millicent. I never made the mistake of showing them to her, but all day at work I did my best to impress, and my worshipping eyes must have had the unswerving fervour of Hitler's. My consolation, when I got things in perspective a bit later – about fifteen years later – was that she would probably not have been interested even if I had looked and sounded less like an aspiring disciple of Christ who had been rejected on grounds of mental instability. She had, after all, recently married a young doctor who called for her at work one day seemingly specifically to convince me of his close physical resemblance to Alain Delon. Perhaps it *was* Alain Delon, whose career was at that time only just starting to boom. Perhaps the reason I thought that he merely looked like Alain Delon was the tears in my eyes. Not that Millicent required anything beyond herself as a stimulus to induce weeping. Merely to glance at her was to feel the tear ducts fill and spill like cisterns after spring rain.

Her eyes would have been too big if they had not been pale blue. The planes of her face were too classically defined for lips so romantically lush, but the clarity of her cheeks showed that there was more life in her than could possibly remain calm – the blood flooded under them like a peach ripening before your eyes. Her straight dark hair was so strong that wisps of it would fight loose from the ribbon tying it back, so that occasionally, without looking up, she would have to lift one long-fingered hand to clear her vision. This movement would bring certain sections of her upper figure into play. There were several opportunities a day to see the whole of her statuesque form in motion. I preferred to avoid these by either closing my eyes or else averting them, lest I emit, as I did on that first afternoon, an involuntary groan of such intensity that Saraj offered me a Beechams Powder. Millicent had the kind of hips known as child-bearing by those people who try vainly to remind us that all these splendours are laid on exclusively for the purpose of reproducing the human race. But it was Millicent's breasts which struck me at the time as constituting unarguable proof that the Man Upstairs was trying to find out how much he could get away with without causing a mass rebellion. Indeed at one point during a mix-up at the coat-rack in the corridor, Millicent's breasts struck me physically. It felt like being run through twice with an angel's tongue. But to arrange another such accident would have caused comment, and anyway ideal-ism shies from reality, even when, especially when, the reality matches the dream. All day and every day I confined myself to dreaming. When Millicent's hand was raised to restore a stray strand of hair, there was a slight shift of the breast on that side. It was enough to make me cram the corner of a questionnaire into my mouth and bite it to stop squealing.

Occasionally, about once every thirty-four minutes on average, Millicent would get tired of coding, put down her pencil, lift both her clenched fists high behind her head, and yawn. As an alternative to swallowing a ques-tionnaire whole I coded furiously, branding female or-phans who lived with foster parents in Wandsworth and studied bookkeeping at the polytechnic as male upper-middle-class Oxbridge history graduates with an interest in blood sports. There is also a possibility that I was trying to impress her with my coding. I was probably trying to make her think: 'My God, can that boy *code*.' In other words, I was acting like a virgin. Hating myself for it too, because I wasn't one, was I? But I was starting to forget what not being one was like, and was not yet experienced enough to know that for any man short of senility or satyriasis, virginity is a recurring condition, and not the worst from which he can suffer, although only self-possession can make it graceful.

Since I had self-obsession instead, I was not best equipped to maintain my equilibrium. Writing badly by night and coding badly by day, I was getting less enjoyment than I should have done out of my first long taste of being alone and paying my own way, or some of it. But not even the most determined cultivation of chaos can prevent the occasional outbreak of order. Having been advised by Robin that the Courtauld Gallery was just around the corner, I began spending some of my lunch-time there. The Italian primitives would probably not have said much to me even if they had been first-rate: my appreciation of painting was fated to work backwards from a starting point in recent times, so as yet I found the Renaissance, when I visited the National Gallery, an elaborate preparation for Rembrandt, whose main achievement in turn was to have done all that could be done with darkness, so that one day the Impressionists would show the same exhaustive virtuosity with light. But the Courtauld's Impressionists and Post-Impressionists *were* first-rate. The great names were represented by only a few paintings each, yet these were capital works without exception. For the first time I got beyond admiring the individual painter and became immersed in the individual painting. There was a comfortable leather bench on which I sat and stared at Manet's girl at the 'Bar of the Folies-Bergère' for half an hour on end, not always in the hope that Millicent would walk in and catch me there looking intense. After the first few weeks the accumulated evidence that she was never going to visit the Courtauld Gallery had become overwhelming.

As with many scatter-brained women her handbag was a bin, out of which she would produce, when the tea-break conversation flagged, one of those cube-shaped paper-back novels by which American authors in elevator shoes take revenge on their country for its having rendered them illiterate. In Millicent's case it was always the same novel, called something like *The Insatiables*. She would take squares of fudge out of the bin and melt them in her lovely mouth while it formed silent words as she slowly read. She is probably still reading that book and I would be surprised if the fudge hadn't taken its toll, although not disappointed. Usually we do not want people to flourish after they have proved that they can live without us, but Millicent was a special case. And to think I never got near her – except when, instead of the fudge, she produced from her bin one of the ten cigarettes to which she rationed herself each day. I would always lean across the table and light it for her. The table was eight feet wide, but before the filter tip of each lucky Dunhill had settled into position between those sumptuous lips I would have lit a match and be sliding across that polished mahogany like a speed skater falling headlong and face downward on the fleeing ice.

My own cigarette ration was more like twenty during working hours, with twenty more each evening. By the time I eventually quit, about twelve years ago, I was smoking eighty cigarettes a day. People who scoff at this figure have never noticed how quickly a true addict smokes a cigarette, so that the burning tip, instead of being a shallow glowing cone, is like a red hot wire. Also you get to the point of having two cigarettes going at the same time, until you reach the terminal stage when you have three of them in your mouth at once, recoiling in sequence like guns in a turret. I finally quit when I found myself at two o'clock one morning assaulting a cigarette machine which had taken my last four coins and given nothing in exchange. The machine will probably never forget my deadly flurry of right uppercuts and left jabs, but that's another story. Even when confining myself to a comparatively moderate forty a day, however, I must have been a spectacle, with butts piling up around me and my beard turning yellow around the mouth. On my right hand, only the little finger was the colour of skin. The thumb and three remaining fingers were a startling mixture of orange-peel and gold leaf. It didn't take a genius to figure out that the nicotine must have been turning me the same colour inside as outside. All it took was someone capable of mature reflection.

More important in the short term, which for a long time remained the only term I could think in, was that the cigarettes ate up a large proportion of the money I had left over after paying the rent and buying the ingredients for my evening meal of bacon and sausages cooked in the fat of a similar meal cooked the evening before. The last duty-free Rothmans was far behind on the horizon, like a ship disappearing towards a more affluent world. For a while I still smoked the same brand, but with tax added to the price they would have been far too expensive even if my first pay packet had not revealed the full meaning of the word 'stoppage'. It meant heart-stoppage. Some form of emergency tax had been imposed until such time as I qualified for a rebate. Presumably one qualified for a rebate by being able, for several weeks consecutively, to read the amount which had been withheld without succumbing to cardiac infarction. This was all a bit much, especially coming on top of the weekly National Insurance slug. I had thought that National Insurance was meant to insure me, but judging from the size of the compulsory contributions the idea was to insure the nation. So I switched to Players No. 6. A lot shorter than Rothmans, they were the tiny kind of cigarette that children smoked at matinees. In recompense my daily consumption shot up to sixty, with consumption sounding like the operative word. If coughing was a sign of literary ability, I would soon be up there, or down there, with Keats and Kafka.

Summer arrived, the job ran out, and the team dispersed, some of them to take an early holiday before starting serious work. Millicent walked out of my life, swaying gently at the hips: a new recruit for the growing army of the untouched, another chapter in the history of what never happened. I took the loss stoically, screaming only when alone. One of those naturally grave young men to whose air of tranquillity I aspired in vain, Robin had impressed me with the seriousness of his enforced exile, something with which voluntary exile has little in common. I was merely on a long holiday. He was banished. But all the more devotedly he studied to be a lecturer in English literature, showing remarkable tolerance for my views on the subject, which he was well aware owed their fluency to a culpable superficiality in the actual business of reading the books. It is never heartwarming, when you are three-quarters of the way through *The Wings of the Dove*, to be told by someone who has read only three pages of it that it is not worth reading. Robin not only mastered his justifiable impatience, he actually helped me line up another casual job, just around the corner in Gordon Square – something about counting up all the foreign students in Britain. But the job didn't start for another two weeks, during which I would be once again flat broke.

Telling people I was on a fortnight's holiday and would soon be drawing pay again, I raised almost enough scratch to smoke and drink continuously, provided I got plenty of sleep during the day. Much of this sleep I got in the parks. I slept in Hyde Park near the Serpentine, St James's Park near the pond, Green Park, Regent's Park and Holland Park. Daringly ranging further afield,

I slept for several hours in the grass at Richmond while deer cropped up to a few feet all around me, so that I woke up looking like a chrysoprase cameo. Most adventurously of all, I slept in the meadow at the Mill in Cambridge.

One of my old Sydney fellow students and drinking mates had already been up at Trinity Hall for a year, reading the second part of the Modern Languages tripos as an affiliated student. During his last summer in Sydney we had been on stage together in the Union Revue, I playing Abdullah Tracy, the Arabian millionaire detective, and he making a show-stopping appearance as the rhythm and blues belly-dancer, Fatima Domino. After the show we would join the Downtown Push at whatever party they had crashed and get drunk enough together to forget the waves of indifference which had emanated from the audience. The last time I had seen him, on the drunken night before he sailed for England, he had been wearing full Push battle order, right down to the suede desert boots worn shiny on the toes. Our faces six inches apart, we had shouted farewell on the understanding that the Poms would never suck him in. Now, in Cambridge, he was suddenly in a three-piece suit and sounded like the Queen broadcasting to the Commonwealth. His new accent cut me off at the knees.

Even with his old accent I would not have found it easy to understand what he was talking about. Apparently there were sound academic reasons why he was still up, when everybody else had gone down. Otherwise he would already have gone down and not come up again until Michaelmas, or Candlemas or possibly Quatermass. But being obliged to stay up was nothing like as bad as being sent down. There was a big difference between being sent down and going down. That was one of the first things one learned when one came up. When I heard him use the word 'one' I began to suspect that he had been drugged, tied to a chair and brainwashed. But after a few pints of brown water in the Eagle, plus a few more in the Little Rose – Pepys's pub, he explained with enthusiasm and difficulty – it was more like old times. He hired a canoe at the Mill and we paddled to Granchester, where a lot of young people were sitting around. These, it was explained to me, were not up. A succession of pints at Granchester was cut short by afternoon closing time, whereupon we paddled back to the Mill. Up at Granchester the church clock had stood at ten to three but down at the Mill it was ten to five. Up, down, up, down. The itinerary was out of Rupert Brooke, the echolalia out of *Four Quartets*, the situation out of hand. On the meadows there were some girls sitting down who were also not up. For a while we lay down and then later on we got up. It was in this condition that I fell into Corpus Christi and looked up at where Christopher Marlowe, no mean piss-artist himself, had had his rooms. I was led into Trinity Great Court as Byron had once led his bear. In the main court of King's I was held steady until the Chapel stopped moving. The sun was gone out of the sky but the twilight was like day, so that the dark, honey-soaked biscuit of the stone – long overdue for the thorough cleaning it has since received – looked like an edible cut-out against the brushed azure. A trembling cut-out. Up, down, up, down. A small old man who looked like E. M. Forster shuffled by. It was E. M. Forster.

That evening we ate in an almost empty hall, called Hall. But the Hall of Trinity Hall was not the same as the Hall of Trinity. Trinity Hall was not a Hall at all. Trinity Hall was a college. This was merely its Hall. It was Trinity Hall's Hall, that's all. I was wearing a borrowed gown which kept tripping me up while I was sitting down. I had to keep getting up to fix it, whereupon I would fall down. Brown water was served by a man in a white jacket who helped me when the potato salad got into the sleeve of my gown. Up at the high table, called

High Table, there were men looking down on us. These men, I was told, were Don's. Don's what? It was agreed that I was too tired to contemplate going up to London until next morning, so I slept that night in my friend's rooms. We went up a set of stairs, called a Stair, and fell down in a set of rooms, called a Set. My companion slept in or near his bed but I was not envious. I was perfectly comfortable with my left arm hooked over the towel-rail and my head in the wash-basin, although every half-hour or so there was a terrible noise, like a man singing the first few bars of '*Celeste Aida*' into a bucket.

6

Statistical Catastrophe

Having seen an old friend fall so conspicuously on his feet should have tipped me off that I was falling on my head. Incredibly this was a fact that I had still not faced. It was finally brought home to me by an episode which strikes me even now as so shameful that I have to struggle, as I begin to tell it, against the urge to hide behind chalk-white make-up and a putty nose. But whereas it is simply good manners to make a story about one's ordinary human failings as entertaining as possible, one's extraordinary human failings require less self-indulgent treatment. What I did next couldn't be glossed over with ten coats of hand-rubbed Duco. I took a job on, mucked it up, panicked and ran. That's the long and the short of it. There was a girl involved, but that makes it worse, because she in no way approved of my behaving badly, and the only reason she couldn't help me behave better was that I didn't listen. Remorse, remorse. But let's not jump the gun.

Once again the job was in Bloomsbury, just around the corner from Woburn Walk, in one of whose bow-windowed little houses W. B. Yeats had once written poetry, and in another of whose bow-windowed little houses Ezra Pound had once played the bassoon. Whether the second activity helped or hindered the first has always remained an open question, but to the inward ear of my imagination this was a mighty conjunction of creativity, as if Goethe and Beethoven, instead of slipping through each other's grasp, had settled down in the same street to write *Faust* as an opera. I couldn't walk past those bow windows without shivering, and indeed still can't. Twenty years ago the shiver was at least partly caused by apprehension. The job had something wrong with it. It was too easy.

My employer was some official outfit called the Association for Commonwealth Institutes, if it wasn't the Institute for Commonwealth Associations. Its headquarters were in the usual Georgian terrace house. From the architectural viewpoint, Bloomsbury had been raped twice, once each by the Luftwaffe and London University. The attack by the University had been the more merciless, but there were still a lot of Georgian terraces left. Few of them, however, were quite so elegant as the one housing the Institute for Associations. With the credit obtainable from friends on the basis of my prospective first week's wages minus stoppages but plus rebate, I bought a pair of black chisel-toed Chelsea boots to go with the Singapore suit. Entering the building, I felt that I needed only a bowler hat and a tightly rolled umbrella to make me look the complete Establishment figure. If I had had the hat, hanging it on the hat-rack in the hall without being rendered temporarily headless by my suit would have entailed a pretty energetic combined jump up and lunge sideways, yet the idea was sound. Even the beard, after suitable attention from a pair of nail scissors, looked like something that might have been approved of by the Navy, instead of fired at on sight.

Once having entered the building, I bent to my task. This I did literally, because the task was spread out on one of those familiar large mahogany tables, except that this time I was on my own. The task was a large chart in which I was to enter, against the names of all the institutions of higher learning in Britain, the number and provenance of all the Commonwealth students attending them. At the end of the scheduled two months, the task would be completed by my tallying the total number of entries, thus to give a set of figures which could be read out by the responsible Minister in answer to a parliamentary question already tabled. A cinch. Nothing to it. All it needed was a level head.

For years after the disaster I tried to convince myself that a level head was something I possessed naturally and that I lost it only because of Pandora. In cold retrospect it becomes apparent that a man with the Medusa touch will wreak havoc whether he has help or not, but at the time of the explosion, and for as long as the debris was falling, I couldn't help believing that the whole débâcle had at least something to do with Pandora's legs. Pandora's legs had the rest of Pandora on top of them, which didn't make things any easier. The man in charge, a nice old thing in a three-piece suit with a watch-chain, had explained the chart, shown me how to analyse the data sheets, made a few sympathetic remarks about how my new shoes must have been hurting, and left me alone. It was all plain sailing for about an hour, and then Pandora opened the door to ask me if there was anything I wanted. Instantly I wanted Pandora. Her severe expression only added to her appeal. Those career-girl glasses were something cruel: when she looked at you it was like having your photograph taken by the police. Their frames were so big that she was getting both your profiles to go with the full face. But her mouth was all the more intriguing for being set in a firm line. From there on down she was Jaeger twinset, pearls and plaid skirt with a safety pin, but it was all put on over a figure twanging with whip-lash energy. Millicent's sensuality, the memory of which now began a rapid retreat into the past, had been languid, passive, receptive. Pandora's was the other thing entirely: avid sinuosity on a hair-trigger. And whereas Millicent's legs had been merely poetic, Pandora's were rhapsodic. They came tapering down out of the hem of that glorified Black Watch kilt like a pair of angels nose-diving with their wings folded, did a few fancy reverse curves of small radius so as to recreate the concept of the human ankle in terms of heavenly celebration, and then swooped at an only slightly less vertiginous angle into a pair of black lacquer stiletto-heeled court shoes with little bows near the toes. Stiletto shoes had come on even further in the previous few months, to the point where prospective airline passengers were asked not to wear them. Airliners kept crashing in the Andes and when the search party finally managed to cut its way through the jungle it would find the usual fuselage full of skeletons, except that at least one of the skeletons would be wearing stiletto shoes which had to be extracted from the metal skin of the pressure cabin with a pair of pliers. Pandora's heels were like that. Looking at her for the first time with roughly the emotions of the Flying Dutchman meeting her namesake, I suddenly and strangely remembered a more than usually weird case study in Havelock Ellis about a man who got his rocks off by lying down and having women stand on his vital areas without removing their buttoned boots. If Pandora were to co-operate in such a venture, there could be no doubt that the experience would prove terminal, but what a way to go. Pinned like a butterfly. This ambiguously disturbing prospect was made even more unsettling by her air of severity. Though she didn't look as if she would be much interested in your pleasure, an interest in your pain was clearly not to be ruled out.

I was maligning her, of course: it was just the glasses. Having foisted one of my fantasies on Millicent, I had immediately set about foisting a different fantasy on Pandora. But there could be no doubt that the detachment of her manner was more effective than a provocation. To indicate that there was nothing I wanted, I raised both hands as if to fend off help, while saying: 'No worries.' What I said came out muffled, but her reply was witheringly clear. 'Is there something wrong with your clothes? What happened to your head just then? You looked like Charles I.' I told her the story of the Singapore suit, a would-be self-deprecating routine which by then, after so much practice, was in a high state of polish. Any normally equipped English-speaking female could be depended upon to laugh aloud at least twice during this comic *tour de force*, but Pandora didn't crack a smile. This was particularly galling in view of the fact that her line about Charles I had been pretty good. Not perhaps a miracle of invention, yet tellingly delivered from the dead pan. Pans didn't come deader than Pandora's pan. I was gibbering. What could I do to break the pack ice on that minatory face?

The answer was nothing, but I didn't find that out before trying everything. There was a Howard Hawks season at the National Film Theatre. I took her to see *His Girl Friday*, one of the funniest films ever made. She sat there like a world champion poker player. Her studied indifference might have had something to do with the way I rolled in the aisle. (Anyone who rolls from side to side in the aisle might be doing so naturally, but to roll up and down the aisle is an affectation.) If that was so, however, why did she agree to go out with me again? And she always said yes to going out, just as she always said no to any form of physical contact. When I asked her if it was the beard she said it wasn't. Then what was it? One night we went to the Royal Court to hear Lotte Lenya sing Brecht and Weill. Lenya's voice was in rags from laryngitis and the tube trains arriving and departing under the theatre sounded like a fault in the earth's crust, but the acrid lilt of 'Surabaya Johnny' proclaimed the inexorability of desire. Pandora invited me back to her flat for coffee. I told myself to stay calm and it would all drop into my lap. It did, too: a steaming hot mug of Nescafé. Nothing else. Perhaps it was a tactical error to give her my standard lecture on the evils of capitalism. I gave her the short version – less than three-quarters of an hour – but before it was half over she was saying 'Really?' in the middle of each sentence as well as at the end. When I tried to kiss her on the way out I rammed her spectacle frames. It was like being thrown against a windscreen.

History was leaving me behind. John Glenn went into orbit but I stayed earthbound. Britten wrote his *War Requiem*. Basil Spence built Coventry Cathedral, which briefly held the title of Most Hideous Building in Britain before the new London Hilton pipped it for top spot. The Mariner unmanned space mission left for Venus. The Moulton small-wheeled bicycle appeared on the streets of London, giving the miniskirts of its female riders a further boost towards the belt. When a girl's tights came towards you on a Moulton, they were making scissor movements at eye level, especially if you were on your knees sobbing with lust. The air was pulsating with libido, but somehow Pandora hadn't heard the news. I knocked myself out trying to impress her. There is no point trying to impress women – if they are listening to you at all, then they are already as impressed as they are ever going to get – but this fact takes some of us a long time to learn and even then it is easily forgotten in the stress of frustration. Pandora wasn't impressed with what I knew. An Oxbridge education had equipped her to say 'Really?' on those occasions when she was told something she didn't know already. When Pandora said 'Really?' it was like being flicked in the face with a wet, sandy towel. Equally clearly she was not impressed with my looks, clothes or earning potential. No doubt it was out of fairness that she always paid her share, yet her manner implied that she was subsidising a gypsy. So there was nothing left to impress her with except a revolutionary new method of calculating the number of foreign students.

Why this did not impress her mystified me at the time.

My formula was a breakthrough in sociologico-statistical methodology comparable to those diagrams by Pareto showing causes and effects all linked up with arrows. With four different coloured pencils I approximated the increment against the asymptotic co-ordinate. The chart looked like Stravinsky's holograph manuscript of *Le Sacre du printemps* overlaid by a computer print-out of the Walt Disney Organisation's payroll. My employer, Mr Niceold Thing – soon, if all went well, to be Sir Niceold Thing – dropped in to see how my work was going and pronounced himself dazzled. 'But doesn't this slow everything down terribly?' he asked. 'Only,' I explained patiently, 'in the initial stages. It takes a few weeks to do the transpositions, but then all you have to do is read off everything in the right-hand column and you get the whole answer in a few minutes.'

He wasn't as convinced as I was, but he needed to be only half as convinced as I was to be convinced enough. Instead of ordering me to forget the new method and just get ahead with the old one, he retreated looking trustful but worried – never a good sign in a commander. He probably blames himself for what happened and I must say that there are moments when I agree with him. They are weak moments. Pandora, after all, told me outright that I was breaking a butterfly on a wheel, or words to that effect. 'Making a meal of it, aren't you?' Without lifting my head I converted the five Sierra Leone students at the Bradfield Polytechnic into a green Greek gamma with a pink circle around it. 'Just put down the tea, smart-arse,' I retorted. It was part of my new plan to relax her with obscene banter. It wasn't working any better than the old plan, but it wasn't working any worse either, which made it a potential step forward.

'Would you like a cake?' she asked with what sounded like less than total indifference to my destiny.

'Sticky cake or crumbly cake?' I riposted, edging the pink circle with yellow.

'No, not cake. *Cake*. Cake-Akela. Thought you might be hot.'

I looked up to see that she had brought two bottles of the familiar American beverage in its sensually draped and fluted bottle. This was tantamount to a love-tryst. I followed it up immediately and once more crunched the bridge of my nose into her spectacle frames. If she had not been turning away as I lunged forward with my eyes closed, the hinge where the ear-piece joined the main frame would not have cracked open and spilled the tiny brass pivot. A long way above me as I crawled around looking for it, she kept saying 'Really' without the question mark, which made it sound even worse.

Getting her back to the mood of relative abandon in which she had voluntarily brought me a fizzy drink took weeks. My first English summer was now at its blazing height. For an hour on end the sun would shine. In the parks at lunchtime the English males would bare their potato-white bodies to what they had heard described as ultra-violet rays. Pandora appeared in a new range of dresses which apparently she usually wore only when in Cannes or Nice with Daddy. When we walked in Lincoln's Inn Fields the allegedly pitiless sunlight did nothing to unfreeze her cryogenic face, but at least it silhouetted her legs through the thin gingham so that I could see the shapely shadows heading upwards. When I tore off my shirt, the remnants of my Australian tan made a remarkable impression on her. No impression. None. In desperation I switched back to the indoor approach and took her to see the Lycergus Cup in the British Museum, hoping that the sunlight slanting through its delicate green and pink calyx would touch some deep, repressed, Dionysian impulse in her Apollonian soul. It didn't.

Not making it with Pandora, I was fatally distracted from the more portentous truth that I was not making it with my job either. By the time the awful facts sank in, it was too late. There was no hope of assembling my multicoloured symbol-scramble into an intelligible order: not in the time available, and probably not within the foreseeable duration of the known universe. Neither was there time to go back and start again with the ordinary method. Somebody normal might just have managed it, but my morale had collapsed. With the parliamentary question only ten days away, I turned up at work, looked obliquely at the chart, sat down and wrote poems. Every time my employer stuck his head through the door, I brusquely assured him that any moment now, with a stroke of a pencil, the scheme would yield its results. Pandora no longer made her daily appearance. Putting my hand on her bottom in the British Museum had been a terminal mistake. She was looking at the Elgin Marbles and for a blessed second I thought that I was feeling them: cool, firm, curved even in their planes. Then her favourite word, only this time with an exclamation mark, echoed through the museum like a polite gun-shot, or a door that had never really been open clicking finally shut.

There was only one honourable course: to go to the boss and make a clean breast of my failure. So I took the dishonourable course. On the third last day before the deadline I did not go to Bloomsbury. I went to Birmingham instead. On the credit side of the ledger – the sole positive entry – may be put the fact that I didn't do a midnight flit from my digs. Fronting up to the landlady fair and square, I paid her a month's notice and no arguments. A committed sherry-drinker who was invariably blotto by eleven in the morning, she failed to recognise me, which made it easier. Toting the cardboard suitcase, wearing the Singapore suit, sweating into the Chelsea boots which already had holes in them, I headed for Euston and the train that would take me north to sanctuary. The ticket cost me the last cash I had, but I was cleaned out in the metaphorical sense only. My soul was heavy with the fluid of a molten spine. After such knowledge, what forgiveness?

7

The Birmingham Decision

Head of the Department of Psychiatric Medicine at the University of Birmingham, Professor William Trethowan had a wife, two teenage daughters, a son in short pants and an unexpected bearded visitor holding a cardboard suitcase. 'What's wrong?' was the first thing he asked. I shrugged. 'What happened to your head just then?' was the second thing he asked, but in a detached manner, not pressing for an answer. He had an apparent lack of concern which people in trouble who found concern inhibiting would seek out, so I was far from being the first unannounced runaway to darken his door. At Sydney University, where I had first met him, his house had been a hostel-cum-clinic for highly strung would-be poets. An eminent English doctor of medicine who talked like George Sanders, played jazz trumpet, was generally interested in the arts and had a wife both keen and competent to produce the first Beckett and Pinter plays Sydney had yet seen – it was a challenging proposition for Australian students who were accustomed to a solid show of philistinism even from the Arts faculty. My neurotic but divinely gifted friend Spencer had arrived for dinner at the Trethowans one April night and not left until August.

I can give Professor Trethowan his real name and occupation because there was nothing professional about our relationship even at this, the lowest moment of my life, when I must have so closely resembled one of the case studies that could never be discussed outside his office. When I asked for refuge and time to think, he gave me both freely, plus unlimited access to his precious collection of old Vocalion 78 rpm records featuring Benny Carter. If I had asked to have my confession heard he would no doubt have granted that wish also, but whether from a Protestant upbringing or an innate suspicion of my own theatricality I have never been able to believe in that particular method of purging a sin. In my experience the sin is still there afterwards. Whenever the late and unlamented Albert Speer said 'I should have known', I always recognised my weaker self staging a carefully underplayed tantrum in which maudlin exhibitionism palmed itself off as atonement. Of *course* he should have known. That was his crime: deciding not to. Yet although I could honestly plead innocent to any charges of mass murder, the relative puniness of my transgression did not alter its absolute reprehensibility. For a while I contemplated emigrating back to Australia. At that time an Australian visiting Britain had all the advantages of British citizenship, including the opportunity to emigrate home again at a cost of only ten pounds sterling. Many of my compatriots who ran out of funds and hope used this escape route. Even as I thought of it, a change in the law closed the loophole for good, as if to ensure that I should not outwit my destiny. So there was nothing left except suicide.

As the last of summer strove tenaciously to keep the potted plants alive in the pedestrian areas of Birmingham's new Bull Ring shopping complex, I would trail my way from one zebra crossing to the next, tour the art gallery, gaze at the Pre-Raphaelites (not as many as in Manchester, but more than enough) and consider the various possible means of my forthcoming voluntary exit. There is something about the Pre-Raphaelites which makes me contemplate self-inflicted death even when my conscience is clear – something to do with the way they managed to predict every shade of lipstick on a modern cosmetics counter. But this time I was definitely, or at any rate pretty seriously, planning to rid the world of my presence. Adopting a mysterious smile which enjoined complicity, I presented my four-volume Nonesuch Shakespeare to the younger daughter and my cherished association copy of *Practical Criticism* to the elder. I was saying goodbye to the treasures I had laid up on earth. Now nothing remained except the final act. When I sat down to write the letter which would explain this decisive step to my mother, however, I had a lot of trouble with the opening paragraph. It wasn't easy to hit the right tone.

There was another difficulty. Either I loved life, or I couldn't take my misery seriously enough. Perhaps there was, and is, a connection. To be incorrigibly ebullient might entail a congenital inability to assess the shambles around us in its correct importance. Since on this occasion the shambles had been wholly caused by me, I could hardly escape being at least shaken. It never came to choosing between the sleeping pills and the slashed wrists, but there was food for deep and severely troubled thought. My first thought, now that I had resolved not to end it all, was of how to get my books back, but on second thoughts I decided to regard their loss as a down payment on the appropriate propitiatory offering to the gods. This matter decided, it began occurring to me that my grand schemes for working by day and writing by night all had a fundamental flaw – my lack of qualifications for working by day. Unless the task was of the simplest and most undemanding, my mind wandered. Even at that stage, after so many years of evidence, I had not yet realised that there could be no task simple and undemanding enough, but at least I now resolved not to take on anything which could not be successfully tackled by a ten-year-old child. I had overestimated the age bracket, but the idea was right.

Another right idea was to negotiate my way back to some sort of institute of higher learning. For the lost soul, the university is the modern monastery. On top of that, it had started to dawn on me that my years as a student at Sydney University had been fruitful in everything except actual study. I needed time to read seriously, and working all day was no more favourable to heavy reading than it was to writing. Also I hadn't been able to get out of my mind a story my Cambridge friend had told me about the poet Gray. It was to do with his epoch-making switch from one Cambridge college to another. At Peterhouse they had made an apple-pie bed for him once too often, so he had crossed the road to Pembroke. That journey of about twenty yards was, apart from one brief visit to a country churchyard, the biggest thing that ever happened to him. I needed to be somewhere where a twenty-yard walk was an adventure and you could spend your life polishing a single elegy. Dreaming of Cambridge should normally have been an activity on a par with my previous plans to take a flat in Belgravia. But strangely enough I had a possible way in, or up. My capacity for wasting time at Sydney University had attracted the amused attention of the Reader in English, George Russell. Humanely learned in Old English, Middle English and the European Middle Ages generally, he had a lot of information to impart; all of which I managed to ignore. I still recollect with shame how, in a seminar, he opened Ernst Robert Curtius's *European Literature and the Latin Middle Ages*, raised his hands above it as if he were breaking communion bread, and called it a great book. The shame springs from the fact that twenty years were to go by before I bothered to find out that he was right. But he must have thought I had promise. Every week Françoise and I were invited to his house and there I was gently but firmly introduced to classical music. In return for being allowed to assail George and his wife Isabel with my Thelonious Monk LPs, I was obliged to at least consider the more accessible quartets of Vivaldi. Always I got dead drunk on George's well-chosen wines. My comportment must have been less brutish than I remember, because he told me – or rather told Françoise, so that she could tell me when I sobered up – to get in touch with him if the day ever came when I wanted to settle down and read seriously, an activity for which he thought I had a considerable, if entirely unexplored, talent. At Pembroke College, Cambridge, they might possibly take me, he ventured, on his recommendation. His own career at the college had been so distinguished, he neglected to add, that even if I turned out to be an utter goof they would still be in profit.

At the time, and for a long time afterwards, I thought nothing of this offer, believing that the cloisters were no framework for a serious artist. But in Birmingham, living on charity, with autumn crowding glumly in and nothing in view except further proof of unfitness for everyday life, the serious artist was ready to think again. So I composed a densely packed airletter to George Russell begging him to get me in out of the cold. It was a carefully phrased effort, a concentrated masterpiece of the epistolary art, and I sincerely trust that he never kept it. He must have acted on it immediately, because within two weeks Pembroke wrote to offer me a place. They had been just as unquestioningly welcoming to Gray, of course, but with better reason, because although he probably cut no great figure as he came sulking across the road with an armful of his bedding, he at least had a few elegies under his belt.

Thus was I offered on a plate what many native-born Britons have to strive for and often in vain – a fact of which not one of them has ever sought to remind me. God knows what George Russell said. He must have told them I had discovered the lost books of Tacitus, squared the circle and was on the verge of developing a unified field theory. But my assumption that to be given a place would ensure an automatic grant proved incorrect. The responsible authorities wrote to say that I could indeed receive a grant, although only after being resident in London for three years. This meant at least two more years of proving myself unemployable. There was nothing for it except to go back south and begin my sentence. Professor Trethowan and his wife, gracious as always, refrained from cheering aloud when I announced my departure. They merely looked very, very happy, as if a weight had been subtracted from their shoulders and added to their refrigerator, which I had been helping their children empty for too long. If it occurred to me that I had been a shameless free-loader, I merely added the realisation to my burden of guilt, as you might toss an apple-core into a skip full of rubbish. 'When you finally get to Cambridge,' said my host in farewell, 'head straight for the Footlights. It's your sort of thing, believe me.' I don't think, at this distance, that he meant my future was on the stage. I think he meant that it wasn't in the cloisters; but I prefer to regard this remark as one more instance of his acute psychological insight. The Viennese essayist Friedrich Torberg once poured out his troubles to Alfred Adler, who told him that with so much going wrong he had a right to feel lousy. Torberg immediately felt marginally, but crucially, better. Bill Trethowan had the same knack. He knew I had a bad conscience and he didn't pretend that it could easily be made good. The gnawing conscience, the agenbite of inwit, helps us know ourselves. Showing an unprecedented measure of dignity, I refrained from putting the agenbite on him for my bus-fare. Instead I took his daughters aside and fixed a price for the books I had already given them. Kisses all round and I was gone, hoping I looked like a devil-may-care vagabond. If only we could really tell what impression we make. Probably there would be no living.

The bus from Birmingham's Digbeth deposited me in

Hammersmith's Talgarth. Digbeth, Talgarth: it sounded like one of those Anglo-Saxon chronicles which mercifully exist only in fragments. I was a stranger in a strange land, a wanderer reduced to his essentials, with only a suitcase for shelter and the light of my red shoes to steer by. Yet fortune, ever ready to rub in the message that what she holds back from the deserving might be given to the undeserving if she is in the mood, chose this moment to smile. There was a party on at Melbury Road. In quick succession I was offered a place to sleep and a job which might have been tailor-made.

My benefactors were dancing together. One of them was Babs, an Australian girl actually living in the top flat of Melbury Road at the time, and the other was one of her several English admirers, a dandruffy man in a crumpled three-piece suit who had trouble getting people to remember that he was called Trevor. His main problem was that nobody understood what he did. Computers were his field and he talked a lot about how they were going to revolutionise the world, to the point that ordinary people would have a computer in the house, and so on. All this would have sounded like nonsense even if he and Babs had not been dancing the Shake while he was saying it. But he had a room for rent in his flat, available as of now. When I asked him where the flat was, it was as if I already knew the answer, and was only seeking confirmation. 'Tufnell Park,' he said. 'Up and coming area.' Babs, who was now twisting while Trevor was shaking, was even harder to hear because she was going up and down instead of just vibrating, but I gathered that a job in one of the Lambeth public libraries would be open from the next Monday and with her recommendation I would be a dead certainty. She had worked there herself the previous year and the librarian would do anything she told him to. Trevor, to whom the same clearly applied, nodded vigorously, but that could have been the music. 'All you have to do is put books on shelves,' shouted

Babs. 'For you, it's tailor-made.' My recent experience of tailors might have warned me, but there was too much noise and too much beer. There was a plastic barrel of it in the kitchen with a little spigot that you could lie under.

Trevor had one of the new Minis. With my suitcase across the back seat and my soused body hanging in the front passenger's seat belt like the corpse of an executed revolutionary, I went back to Tufnell Park. Nor was it even a different part of Tufnell Park. Trevor's flat was just around the corner from where I had been before. I felt like a rat going back to Tobruk, to a place I returned to only in order to be bombed out of. Page 45 of the *London A–Z* had become my map of the world. But my allotted room couldn't have been cosier. Beside the bed there was space for the suitcase if it stood upright. There was also space for me if I stood upright, as long as I stood upright on the bed. Time for that tomorrow. The problem now was to lie down without getting hurt. I started by kneeling and then did the difficult next bit by twisting myself sideways so that my mouth hit the pillow at an angle which allowed breathing. You can tell when it works because you wake up again next morning.

On the weekend before my new job started I paid two important calls. The first of them was to say goodbye to Pandora, who told me that she was under the impression I had said goodbye already. It transpired that she and Niceold, to save the Minister from parliamentary embarrassment, had worked together for two days and a sleepless night in order to accomplish what I had failed to do in two months. When I laughed nervously at this information she used her favourite word with no emphasis at all, like a death knell tolled by a cracked bell underwater. I backed out on all fours with a last, long, longing, hopeless look at her intractable ankles. The second call was on Joyce Grenfell and wasn't much more successful. My account of recent events drew the bare minimum of appreciative laughter. Never one to preach, she none the less made it known that in her view those who regarded themselves as gifted had fewer, not more, excuses for behaving badly. Characteristically she had seen through at a glance to the centre of my self-indulgence. Satan's opening remarks are almost always about how talented we are. As I left her, I was already chewing over the implications. They were too many to swallow that day or, as I can now see, that year or that decade, and perhaps the lesson has not fully sunk in even yet.

There were several Lambeth libraries, of which the one with the putative sure-fire job for me was in Brixton. A bus from Holloway Road went straight there, taking only nine years for the journey. By the time I got there I would have needed another shave, so the beard was a plus. Clad in the Singapore suit, I evidently impressed the librarian, whom I will call Mr Volumes because at this distance I can't remember anything about him except the way he spoke. He spoke very loudly. Even for a road-worker wielding an unjacketed pneumatic drill he would have spoken loudly, but in a librarian his voice was truly startling. In all other respects he was a shambling buffer but then this stentorian voice came out. 'YOUNG BARBARA SAID YOU WERE JUST THE MAN. WAS SHE RIGHT? EH? EH? WHAT?' I did a lot of nodding, got the job, was shown out of the office into the reading room, and stepped on the delicately tapering right hand of Lilith Talbot, who was kneeling down to shelve some books with a lithe grace never employed on shelving books up to that time.

In Sydney, Lilith, the glamour girl of the Downtown Push, had memorably divested me of my virginity, something which had been of no use to anyone. As the personal property of the notorious gambler Emu Coogan she had not been able to go on with our affair – or that was what she had said, perhaps letting me down lightly. But now, in despair at Emu's continued indebtedness to the standover men (apparently he had spent a night chained upside-down to one of the Mosman wharf pilings, listening to the rising tide) she had run away to England. Her intention was to recuperate from years of stress. Instantly I saw my own role in her recuperation.

She didn't see it the same way, so I had to reconcile myself to our renewed friendship remaining chaste for the immediate future. Meanwhile I did everything I could to ensure that my presence bulked large in her life. During the morning shelving session we would shelve as a team. 'CANOODLING AGAIN, YOU TWO?' Mr Volumes insinuated gleefully, whereat the sleeping tramps at the reading table would come up out of their chairs mumbling automatic apologies. This was embarrassing but it helped get the idea into Lilith's head. Also I took her out a lot, principally to the National Film Theatre. She sat through a whole Vincente Minnelli season, each film prefaced by a long free lecture from me, delivered on the bus. Walking back across Waterloo Bridge in the first fogs of winter, I would deliver a further monologue concerning the finer points of what we had just seen. She seemed appropriately grateful for all this instruction, which she was getting for almost nothing. Out of my weekly wage, after stoppages, I paid for all my own cigarettes and cider, on top of most of my rent. All Lilith had to do was buy the NFT tickets and provide the occasional small loan when we dined out together.

Dining out meant shepherd's pie and bitter at the Anchor, Bankside. The Anchor was a little sooty brick Georgian pub on the Embankment. You could sit on the wall outside and look across the river to St Paul's. The tiny house from which Christopher Wren had once done the same thing was a few yards along on the left, on the same site as a previous house where Catherine of Aragon had spent the night on her way upriver to marry Henry VIII. Lilith and I sat there in our duffle-coats looking out over the Whistlerian nocturne, with no sound in the cold air except the muffled drunks in the pub, the dimpled

85

gurgle of the tide turning, the chugalug of the barges, and the slurred drone of my voice telling her about the genius of Arthur Freed and the exact difference between Fred Astaire and Gene Kelly. Framed in the hood of her duffle-coat, her angelic face looked as if it were receiving a revelation. It always did, of course. Long practice at listening to the gratuitous political lectures of the Downtown Push had taught her to yawn with her mouth closed, with no tell-tale flaring of her poetically sculpted nostrils.

My campaign to get Lilith back into bed would have run into trouble even had she been compliant, because there was nowhere to go. Her bed-sit in Maida Vale was on the fourth floor of a red-brick terrace house inhabited on the first three floors exclusively by landladies. It must have been some sort of landladies' training college: they were all in there, learning how to pick up the sound of illicitly creaking bedsprings and stockinged male feet on the stairs. They had echo-sounders and infra-red detectors. The layout *chez* Trevor was theoretically permissive but in practice hopeless. Trevor's large room contained Trevor's electronic gear, Trevor's weirdo junior-scientist friends, and Trevor. He slept there on a convertible divan: one of those things that doesn't look much like a sofa, but after you fiddle with it for a while it doesn't look much like a bed. To uproot Lilith from polite drinks in the living-room and lead her off into my adjacent roomette could be for one purpose only, especially when you considered that unless we climbed straight away into my bed we would have to squat on it like Indians. After a gallon or so of Woodpecker the obviousness of such a move might be lost on me, but Lilith was not only sober, she was, like all genuinely sexy women, decorous. Anyway, even this slim possibility disappeared when Trevor evicted me. Accurately pronouncing me a defaulter on my payments, he rented the room to a girl folk-singer. I could kip on the floor of his

86

living-room until I had found somewhere else. He was very nice about it, but also very firm. I think he had hopes of getting somewhere with the folk-singer, who sang the standard Weavers repertoire with a Roedean accent. Her name was Ninette and that was the name of her LP: *My Name is Ninette*. She made semi-regular appearances on the Bernard Braden show on the BBC and was thus well enough off to afford a new inner-spring mattress to go on top of the one provided by Trevor for what had previously been my bed. The mattress came wrapped in a 16-ply paper bag. Autumn had by now become winter in all but name, Trevor's fan-heater did more for his bed than for my area of the floor, and the insulating properties of the paper bag were obvious. So I moved into it.

8

The Man in the Brown
Paper Bag

In Trevor's living-room, my suitcase against the wall
served as a headboard. Folded clothes made a pillow.
Beyond, into the centre of the room, stretched the brown
paper bag, forming my bed. Wriggling into it took some
time, but once inserted I could settle down in comparative
warmth for a long night of turning from one side to the
other. It was the hardness of the floor which compelled
frequent movement. A lot of this I could do in my sleep,
because my body, albeit much abused, was still young
and supple, and I have always had Napoleon's gift of
falling asleep at will, although unfortunately it has not
always been accompanied by his gift of waking up again.
The problem resided not in how the hardness of the floor
affected my sleep, but in how the noise the paper bag
made affected Trevor.

As he lay there in the darkness on his enviably luxur-
ious convertible divan, it was as if, somewhere nearby, a
giant packet of crisps was being eaten by one of those
cinema patrons who think that they are being unobtrusive
if they take only a few crisps at a time and chew them
very slowly. When Trevor could bear no more he would
switch on his modernistic tubular bedside light, wake me
up and tell me to be quiet. Invariably I would discover,
upon waking, that my bladder, which was already show-
ing signs of being weakened by the steady inundation of

cider, demanded emptying. So I had to get out of the paper bag, go away, pee, come back and get back in, thus creating a double uproar. When Trevor switched his light off again I would lie there trying not to move. Only a dead man or a yoga adept can keep that up for more than twenty minutes. Judging that Trevor was asleep again, I would essay a surreptitious turn to one side, making no more noise than a shy prospective bride unwrapping a lace-trimmed silk nightgown from its tissues. This movement completed, for a long time I would lie there, inhaling and exhaling as shallowly as possible and waiting until the sound of Trevor's steady breathing deepened into the second level of sleep. Only then would I make the necessary full turn on to the other side. A man tearing up a thin telephone directory while wading through dead leaves would have been hard put to be so silent. But if, after these manoeuvres, I dropped off to sleep, it was inevitable that an involuntary shift of weight would sooner or later produce the full effect of a large, empty cardboard box being attacked by a flock of woodpeckers. I can be sure of this because sometimes the noise woke me as well.

Even after the student-codifying catastrophe and the subsequent agonising reappraisal, my powers of self-deception were still in healthy shape, but it was not easy to convince myself that mere lack of sleep lowered my performance at the library. I preferred to think that it was the frustration caused by not sleeping with Lilith. Having convinced myself of this, I did my best to make her see reason. In no sense of the phrase was she having any. Probably she had already guessed that I was an irredeemable incompetent. Certainly Mr Volumes had rumbled me early on. The evidence was hard to miss. I always arrived late. Oliver Goldsmith, accused of the same thing, pointed out that he always left early. Lacking his self-confidence, I merely looked sheepish. 'YOU MUST KEEP TIME, YOU KNOW,' Mr Volumes told

me and the rest of the borough. Lilith had been trans-
ferred to another branch so there was nothing exciting to
look at except the tramps who came in to get out of the
cold. They would sit at the big leather-topped table
pretending to read *Country Life* but it was obvious that
the blood-bag eyes couldn't focus on anything except a
bottle of methylated spirits or a tin of boot polish. You
could make bets with yourself about which disease they
would succumb to first, cirrhosis or gangrene. Once a
month they were rounded up and hospitalised so that
their socks could be removed surgically. Skin ingrained
with dirt has the anomalous effect, in the right light, of
looking expensively tanned, as if by the Riviera sun: an
observation which, once I had made it, depressed me
deeply. But the real killer was boredom. Stamping the
cards of borrowers, I ran out of answers for the little old
ladies who wanted to know if they had already read the
book they were thinking about taking out. The smart
ones used a personalised coding system. One of them
would put a small inked cross on page 81 of every book
before bringing it back, so that later on in the library she
could turn to that page and, if she saw her mark, be
reminded not to take the book out again. Another would
draw a circle in red pencil around the last word on page
64. There were hundreds of them at it all the time. If you
picked up a book by Dorothy L. Sayers or Margery
Allingham and flicked through it, you would see a kaleido-
scope of dots, crosses, blobs, circles, swastikas, etc. It was
interesting but not interesting enough. When I met Lilith
in the evening, I complained about having trouble con-
centrating. She advanced the theory that for someone
whose destiny was to read and write books there could
be no profit in being obliged all day to do nothing except
pick them up and put them down. I took some comfort
from this advice, although the historic evidence should
have suggested that it was fallacious. Jorge Luis Borges
and Archibald MacLeish had each pursued a successful

literary career while working as a librarian. Philip Larkin was currently doing the same, although I didn't know that. Admittedly Proust had been a disaster as a librarian but that was mainly because, instead of turning up late, he never turned up at all. When Mr Volumes began hinting, in his subtle way, that I might think of pursuing a similar course, I did my long perfected number of resigning one step ahead of the boot.

Jobless in winter in a paper bag. My discomfiture had a Miltonic ring to it. But now that I was merely working through a sentence towards the day of release, defeat was easier to shrug off, or even to cherish as a token of my rebellious nature. There is also the possibility that I was clinically certifiable at the time. Sex starvation was in its downhill phase and something had gone seriously wrong with my teeth. The half-dozen of them that I had already lost didn't hurt, but those remaining in my head rarely did less than give a sharp twinge when I sucked anything – air, for example. Under Lilith's influence I was now attempting to vary my egg, bacon and sausage diet with the occasional helping of steamed greens, but the treatment was a holding operation at best. The connection between the teeth and the brain is intimate and potentially devastating: that much I knew. But you wouldn't catch me going to a dentist. I was too smart for that.

Breathing carefully through the nose – never an easy trick for a chronic sinus sufferer – I auditioned for a new job at a light metal-work factory off the Holloway Road. The supervisor wore a grey lab coat, had a short back and sides haircut polished with a buffing wheel, and favoured blunt speech. 'I'll speak bluntly,' he rapped. 'Don't like your general appearance. Don't like the beard. Don't like the fingernails. Should have worn a suit, not that jacket. Shouldn't wear a jacket like that unless you're in the army. If you have to wear a jacket like that, should wear it tomorrow, not to your interview. Interview, you should be standing up straight, not slouching like that.

Shouldn't be smoking. I'm not smoking. Why are you? Hope we won't be seeing those shoes again . . .' The roar, clank, thump and *chong chong* of the stamping machines out on the factory floor drowned some of this out but not enough. I listened stunned, which was obviously the desired reaction, because I was taken on, as a general workman, at nine pounds a week before stoppages. Young British-born readers with qualifications but no job will doubtless wince to read of an immigrant with a job but no qualifications. All I can say is that things were different then. The economy was already collapsing but everybody thought the noise was bustle.

With proof of my employed status I found new digs around the corner from Trevor's, in Tufnell Park Road proper. Since it was by now clear that Tufnell Park was my Berlin and my Paris, it was only fitting that I should become resident in its Kurfürstendamm or Champs-Elysées. From the awe-inspiring single-storey edifice of Tufnell Park tube station, Tufnell Park Road swept down majestically for half a mile until it met Holloway Road in a *carrefour* blazing with the glamorous white light of the launderette. At No. 114 I was exactly half-way down the road, and thus equidistant from the only two points of interest. My room was in the basement, with a window opening not so much on the back garden as under it, so that I looked out into a cross section of the earth. But the rent was a more than reasonable thirty shillings a week. In fact it was a snip. Mrs Bennett had not kept up with the times. She was eighty plus and walked with a stoop, which meant, since she was not very tall in the first place, that I often didn't see her before falling over her.

Not seeing her was made easier by the darkness. Her connections with the outside world had been broken on the day when her fiancé sailed away to the Middle East on the same ship as Rupert Brooke. Out there he had suffered the same fate, but without writing any poems. Understandably the modern world had ceased to interest her from that moment, and she had declined to keep up with its inventions, including any light-bulb more powerful than forty watts. The chintz furniture was well dusted but so faded that it was virtually monochrome. No doubt it was all still a riot of colour to her eyes. In the corridors and on the staircase it would have been easier to find one's way by the weak light of the frosted bulbs if only the wallpaper had been a brighter colour. But it was all brown: brown on brown with dark brown wooden trimmings. Sometimes through the layers of varnish you could see the ghost of a William Morris print, like jungle under a flooded river full of mud. Once, while she was waiting, it must have been a bright little house he would have been glad to come home to. Then she went on waiting without an object and it all turned dark. I could sympathise, but things got very tricky on the stairs, which I had to spend a certain amount of time groping up and down because the toilet was on the floor above. If you ran into her in the dark, no matter how slowly you were going, it usually meant a tumble. For her a fall would probably have entailed multiple fractures, but she was so low down that she acted as a fulcrum. It was always the rest of us – everyone in the house at some time or other – who took the dive. This wasn't so bad if you were going upstairs at the time, but if you were heading in the opposite direction it could involve a sudden plunge into the brown void, with a good chance of cracking your head against a skirting-board the colour and consistency of petrified gravy.

With its narrow bed, single-bar radiator and burnt umber decor, my little room was an unlikely setting for happiness, yet Lilith took one look at me in my new context and immediately granted the favours so long withheld. Perhaps she had been touched by the spirit of Christmas. The snow began early that year and a good deal of it had already occupied the top half of the vista through my window, above the half filled with dark earth.

She had come a long way by bus to cook me my weekly lifesaving meal of liver and greens. I was knackered from a hard day in the factory. Also, chary of the effect that the cold air had on my bared teeth, I wasn't doing much talking. This was probably the key factor. Eloquence might get you started with a woman but it is often taciturnity which seals the bargain. Shakespeare has a line about it – in *Henry IV, Part 1*, I think. Those who can rhyme their way into a lady's favour do always reason themselves out again. Not being able to say anything, I couldn't say the wrong thing, which left Lilith, undistracted by importunities, free to decide that in such a depth of winter there was no further point in leaving her beautiful body lonely. There is also a slim chance that I was an irresistible object of pathos, but experience suggests that even the warmest and most generous woman can be moved to tears of compassion without feeling impelled to take off her clothes.

The only real explanation, however, is that I got lucky, not only then but for the rest of my life. Right through that epic of a winter she came to me several times a week. The first love affair I had had which lasted long enough for me to get used to it, it did wonders for my confidence. It probably did wonders for my arrogance, too: her queenly bearing could not, as I recall, prevent my taking her for granted unless she issued the occasional verbal reproof. Innate tolerance – plus, no doubt, vivid memories of Emu Coogan's impecuniosity – made her slow to remonstrate, so I got away with what seemed a lot even at the time, and strikes me in retrospect as something close to white slavery. When I packed her off home on the last bus it was only common sense to give her the poems I was sending out, each batch of them accompanied by a folded self-addressed envelope and placed inside another envelope addressed to an editor. To expect her not only to post the letters but to buy the stamps for each envelope was possibly a bit much. She did it without complaining. Hearing no protest, I took everything and gave nothing.

Some stupidities only time can cure. What could be gained by experience I gained then; or the essentials of it anyway, and the deep self-doubt that inhibits and cripples was obviated at an early stage. Which is not to say that I was permanently immunised against all anxiety. In future liaisons, that particularly humiliating version of impotence known as first night failure was always to be a hazard. But when it struck, it did so in perspective, as an embarrassment rather than an affliction. All it means, if you wilt that way with a lady, is that you haven't yet really met her. You're not trying to make love to a woman, you're trying not to miss an opportunity. I have heard men say that such a thing has never happened to them. The claim, I think, speaks as much against their imaginations as for their virility, but no doubt they are telling the truth. The truth might even redound to their credit: never to be unmanned could be a sign of manhood. Those of us who can't plausibly make the same boast have at least some comfort. We find out the hard way, if that's the appropriate phrase, whether the lady has a forgiving soul. Since no other kind of woman is worth getting mixed up with, the man who crumples at the first sign of impatience should be glad to consider himself forewarned, if not forearmed.

In this case the question became academic after the first evening, and for a long winter that should have been a disaster I put on satisfaction like a weightlifter putting on muscle. Without Lilith I might have been not just unhappy, but dead. The winter deepened into the worst since 1947, then the worst since the year after the Great Fire, then the worst since the last Ice Age. The cleared snow formed long ridges at the sides of the roads. These ice ridges turned dark with dirt: burial mounds for long ships, they were pitted like breeze blocks. With thousands of tons of water lying around in frozen form, the anomalous consequence was a water shortage. So many pipes burst that the system just packed up. You had to draw your household water from a stand-pipe in the street. The residents of 114 Tufnell Park Road took turns to do this on behalf of Mrs Bennett, whose only recorded journey outside the front gate was instantly defeated by the frozen snow-ridge at the road's edge. It was taller than she was. After gazing for a while into that threatening escarpment of refrigerated lucent suet, she turned back bewildered.

Bewildered and coughing. Many old people died younger than they should have, that winter. If they were poor they died of hypothermia. If they were well enough off to keep their radiators going full-time, it was the acid fogs that got them. The fogs, the last great fogs that London was ever to see, were Dickensian epics through which I groped home from work each evening, lucky to be young and mobile. The bus that brought Lilith to me would arrive an hour late, its headlights diffused by the fog into opalescent radiance. Mrs Bennett was always glad to see Lilith and usually arranged to be on the stairs so that we could both fall over her. But soon her cough confined her to her room. For a while I was mildly afraid that she had withdrawn because of the shock induced by my poems, which she had asked to see – or had at any rate agreed to be shown – yet had obviously found to be not quite the sort of thing she had grown used to at the time when dear Rupert was into cleanness leaping. Eventually her cough became audible even through the ceiling and thus disabused me of my typically solipsistic notion. You had to be above a certain age to cough like that but anyone who qualified could be sure that there would be nothing temporary about the affliction. Once it started there was only one way of stopping it. Each droplet of fog had a molecule of sulphuric acid attached. The fog looked romantic if your beautiful girl-friend had stepped off a bus and was materialising out of it towards you with the dark outline of her duffle-coat taking shape against the nacreous cloud. To the old people it was breath-taking in a different way. Mrs Bennett was only one of the many who tried to hide from it in the bedroom. But the mist with the sharp taste got in through the old warped door jambs and the place where the window sash would no longer sit square.

Even had she been in sight she would probably still have been out of mind. Her star lodger was too busy being the horny-handed proletarian and tireless young lover. Actually the demands of the first component of this dual role often threatened to inhibit my achievements in the second. After a night spent shivering – if Lilith had been there, my room seemed colder than ever after she was gone – I arrived already tired at the machine shop, where the warm air that would otherwise have been welcome was offset by the continual uproar. The machines were devoted to taking $6' \times 4'$ sheets of metal and punching or drilling various patterns of holes in them. Punches went CHUNK CHUNK and drills went YERK YERK. An acre of machines doing both these things produced a clamour which one's ringing ears might have analysed as CHUNK YERK CHUNK YERK if one's body had not been vibrating. Physically walking on air from the interminably reiterated percussion, I heard the sound as CHU-CHU-CHUNK (CHERK YUNK!) YER-YER-YERK (UNK UNK!) ERK ERK, or sounds to that effect. The machine operators, who had been doing the same sort of work since the Second World War or even earlier, watched the flow of cutting oil and the glittering spillage of metal waste with understandable indifference. Once upon a time the perforated plates had been going into Lancaster bombers and there was point to the work. A team from *Picture Post* had come to take photographs of them cheerfully doing their bit. Now the perforated plates were going into the backs of slot machines that sold Kit-Kats and packets of Smiths

Crisps. Alienation, as defined by the young Marx but better described by the older William Morris, was a palpable presence. Where Marx and Morris had both been wrong, however, was in the assumption that men alienated from their labour must necessarily be denatured. The machine-operators all drove second-hand but immaculately kept Rovers or Riley Pathfinders and had enough spare cigarettes to 'lend' me about a packet a day between them. I was the alienated one and opium was my religion.

My job was to help a man called Fred load as-yet-unperforated metal plates of specified gauge on to a trolley, wheel them to the machines, unload them in sequence, load the finished plates and wheel them back to the racks in which they were stored vertically until shipment. At the beginning and end of this chain of events there was a mildly thrilling moment when Fred picked up and put down the heavier plates by means of a Ferris hoist which ran on a rail in the roof. It was controlled electrically from a hand-set. Fred pressed the buttons on the hand-set and I steadied the plates so that they didn't swing around and swipe anybody. You couldn't call Fred's job skilled labour, so as his assistant I scarcely rated as a dogsbody. This situation was made no easier by Fred's personality. A dedicated racist, he lurked outside the machine-shop door at lunchtime so that he could shout 'ANY COCONUTS?' to the West Indian girls in transit between the steam laundry and the greasy spoon. Even worse, from my angle, he liked to shout racist jokes to me while we were working. He had a theory that all Australians were descended from Aborigines, and that any Australian immigrant into Britain was therefore part of the universal black conspiracy to deprive the British working class of employment. Compounded by the Wagnerian banging and jangling, his sentiments had the same effect on me as the iron band tightening around Cavaradossi's head. Fred's first word was always 'EAR!', by which he meant 'Here!' He kept yelling that until I paid attention. 'EAR! (CHU-CHU-CHUNK) THIS JEW (CHERK YUNK!) ANNA NIG-NOG (YUNK CHERK!) SO EASE ALL BLACK FROM A BOO POLISH (YER-YER-YERK) . . .' Fred didn't put me off the cockney accent, which had already influenced my own, no doubt with ludicrous results. But he would have gone a fair way towards putting me off the proletariat, if I had really believed that it existed. In fact my belief in such things was only theoretical, and even the theory was a fag-end. It had always been transparently obvious to me that there could be no such thing as the masses. There were only people. Even Fred was unique. That was the awful thing about him.

Thus the little factory chuntered on, with Fred and me pushing and pulling our trolley endlessly around its inner perimeter. Meanwhile the rest of the country was gradually coming to a standstill. For some reason which nobody has ever been able to figure out, the British consider themselves to be living in a tropical climate into which any intrusion of snow, no matter how brief, is always regarded as Freak Weather Conditions. The railways, for example, are invariably brought to a halt by any snowfall heavy enough to make the rails show white instead of silver. The drivers in their Hawaiian shirts and dark glasses climb down from their cabins and quit. The trains are not allowed to move again until the commuters have had a day's rest and the tabloid newspapers – even more cretinous than the Australian equivalents – have had a chance to run headlines about the Freak Weather Conditions. (BRR! SAYS BR: IT'S SNOW-GO!) It will be understood, then, that in the winter under discussion the trains vanished for weeks on end. So did most of the livestock. The sheep were so far down that the army was using echo-sounders to find them. Then somebody had to look for the army. It would have been a good story if it had ended at the proper time. But it all went on and on. History, however, has to be truly disastrous before it impinges on your personal odyssey. For me, with my new assurance, the snow was just a backdrop. Secure within, I was looking outwards for the first time.

The owner of the business arrived in a Bentley to tour the shop-floor, his blazered school-age son in attendance. They paraded like royalty, with their hands behind their backs. Only the blunt-spoken supervisor got his hand shaken. It was because his hand was clean. In Australia the air would have been thick with first names. I really was in another country, an observer as flabbergasted by exotic ritual as those first Portuguese in China whose astonished narrative stands out even in Hakluyt's vast codex of the strange. Fascinated, I neglected to steady a batch of steel plates which Fred had just picked up with the hoist. The swinging load knocked him backwards off his feet and on to the trolley, where he lay pondering the implications while the plates shook themselves out of the grip of the hoist, crashed to the concrete on their edges a few inches from his head, and, considerately tilting away from him – instead of, as they might equally well have done, towards – accumulated thunderously on the floor like playing cards in Valhalla. At this point, but for an entirely unconnected reason, the supervisor cut the power in the machines. The owner wished to address his work-force. The clangour stopped with a reverse shock, an inburst of sound, a downroar. Fred, never quick at adjusting to circumstances, was still yelling. '. . . UCK-ING NIG-NOG GIT, YOU'RE AFTER MY JOB!' The owner and his son left hurriedly, even as the blunt-spoken supervisor headed towards me, his eyes narrowed with purpose.

9

Solvitur acris James

Out in the countryside, the corpses of sheep and the hulks of abandoned trains emerged from the melting snow. Spring came to Tufnell Park. It was too late for Mrs Bennett, whose cough had already stopped by itself. Not going to her funeral was a sin of omission easily committed – all I had to do was not ask the precise time it would take place. Also I was busy looking for work. But my conscience was uneasy at the time, and although it never became exactly inflamed on the subject I can still say that my dereliction lived with me as a matter for regret. Perhaps I had been put off death at an early age. Certainly I had a revolutionary socialist's contempt for ceremony, which I construed as empty posturing, and never more so than when the chief participant was, as in this case, dormant. Nowadays I set much less store by my independence of mind, and indeed doubt whether it really exists. Yeats's question about custom and ceremony has at last sunk home. In those days I was either a different man or – something even harder to understand and absolve – a glib version of the same one. The old lady had not only been kind and gracious, she had taken positive delight in the idea that the feckless young writer under her roof had been so thoroughly compromising such a well brought-up girl. One of those rare people who, having missed out on a blessing, are glad instead of bitter to see it conferred on others, Mrs Bennett in death deserved something better from me than the cold shoulder. But she was dealing with someone impatient of mere formalities.

So was Lilith, who wanted to be married. If she had wanted to marry me I would probably have panicked, because a sound instinct told me that I was far from ready. But she wanted to marry Emu, which gave me an opportunity to be peeved. She made the announcement after we had seen *Les Enfants du paradis*. 'If all the people who live together were in love,' said Baptiste, 'the Earth would shine like the Sun.' Lilith had been my Garance. 'When I want to say yes, I can't say no.' How lucky I had been to meet my woman of the world and find it all so easy. Lilith, no less lovely than Arletty, sat beside me, looking as happy in the reflected light as a woman could who had just paid two bus-fares, bought two cinema tickets, and was about to pay for two bus-fares more. All the way home on the slow bus past the now shrinking roadside ranges of dribbling black mousse I explained the significance of what we had just seen, how it was all an idyll. In my little room she took me to her with special tenderness, which should have told me that this had been an idyll too, and must now end. Typically, though, I had to be told what I might have guessed.

Hypocritical jealousy is more enjoyable than the genuine article but I still managed to work myself up into a state. Lilith, however, remained calm. Her mind was already on its way home, and soon her body followed it. The time had come for her to be married, so she went where it would happen. It was as if her mission in my life had been completed. She had got me through the winter without my succumbing to vitamin deficiency: my gums were purple only when I smiled, and I couldn't do much of that even in spring, lest the air get at my teeth. She had also got me through that dangerous second stage of virginity, the stage in which we are only technically no longer chaste, and callow anxiety is compounded by a little learning. I still had a lot more to find out about women, but I was on the right track. It was only much later that I could be sure of this, however, because there is a wrong track which runs beside the right track for a long way.

Released from stability, which youth finds hard to bear even when beneficial, I was suddenly mobile, like the unfrozen landscape. The whole country woke up to an ecstasy of self-consciousness. There were political scandals, quasi-satirical television programmes, hit singles to make the dead dance, and the rise of the miniskirt to ever less prudent lengths of shortness. Cabinet Ministers were disgraced for love, thugs robbed a mail-train and were hailed as heroes, unmasked traitors were admired for their complex personalities, the harlot's cry from mews to mews had the exultant confidence of Callas singing '*Casta diva*', and the Beatles mouthed and mimed to fame in screaming theatres whose seats had to be heat-dried afterwards because they were soaked with the love-juices of pubescent girls. Urgent messages of change came from everywhere, the most insistent of all from my teeth. With my bad conscience blacked out by stabbing pains from molars and incisors, I went on National Assistance to tide me over. When the assessor came to look at me in my room I sat opposite him in the brown darkness with my mouth closed, making signs of need with eloquent hands. Touched, or afraid of infection, he signed the papers and skedaddled.

At a Melbury Road party I met an Australian dentist who impressed me by being able to tell I had toothache by the way I was dancing. He was dancing himself at the time, opposite a wonderfully proportioned girl from Curl Curl. She had a freckled face and a jersey miniskirt whipping softly around her hand-span waist to the sensual pulse of John Lennon's rhythm guitar. She was a red rag to a bull. 'Flash me the fangs for a sec,' said the dentist, matching her step for step as she trod successively on imaginary cigarette butts. 'Shit a brick, you'd better get down to see me pronto.' Next morning – still drunk from the night before or I never would have made it – I arrived at his surgery in Shoreditch to be greeted by the girl from Curl Curl, who turned out to be not only the receptionist but the nurse. She performed this double function in a white uniform of mini length, with white patterned tights below. Her employer, whose name was Barry, conformed in every respect to the paradigm Australian dentist I had been warned against, down to and including the 3.8 Jaguar parked outside. For the English chattering classes, stories about Australians had begun to serve as a mild form of licensed anti-Semitism, a function they retain. One of the stories then current was about the typical Australian dentist who spent a year in London pulling every tooth in sight, thereby defrauding the National Health and making possible the purchase of a 3.8 Jaguar, in which he and his beautiful nurse then decamped to the south of France and retired. Barry had the car and the beautiful nurse but in other ways he didn't fit the stereotype at all. For one thing, he showed no urge to extract any teeth that were not already an obvious lost cause. Instead he fought to save them, despite my generous offer to surrender them without a struggle. 'Nar,' said Barry, 'you don't want to lose that eye tooth. I'll just kill the nerve and go down the hole into the root. Give her a good cleaning out. Nothing a cavity likes more than a good probe, right, Noelene?' If you wonder how I can recall the way Barry talked, it's because trauma etches the memory. Freud's theory of repression is doubtless right – how could we tell if it was wrong? – but in my case it ceases to apply when the subject turns to teeth. Back almost to the beginning of my life, I can remember everything that happened at the dentist's. Mostly what happened was my imagination running out of control, but that made the experience no less frightening. While writing the first volume of this work I was not yet ready to face the full degrading facts of my dental history. I think that by now I can handle it, but if you get the impression in the next few paragraphs that their author is looking into the pit of his own nature, you will probably be right.

It started in Kogarah when I was about seven years old. That dentist, whose own teeth weren't much of an advertisement, should never have told me that the extraction of my abscessed molar wouldn't hurt. It did, distinctly. I felt betrayed, and received no comfort from the dentist, who had received a squirt of pus in the eye. Outrage at his perfidy motivated me to a brilliant career of truancy which ensured that I did not visit any dentist again until all my remaining first teeth were extracted in one go, under gas. When I woke up I was given limitless lemonade and ice-cream as a reward for bravery. In fact my bravery, after a week's delaying tactics including a furniture-fracturing tantrum, had consisted of agreeing to accompany my mother to the surgery on a bus instead of in the police car which she had indicated would otherwise have to be called in. But the Shelley's lemonade was balm to the plundered gums and the Street's ice-cream was a portent of all the sweet things I would now be able to eat when my mother wasn't watching. The Jaffas, Fantails, and Minties which had extracted so many of my first teeth with such precision now riddled my second teeth with cavities. Since I would rather have suffered tooth-ache than go for a check-up, the sweet things got an uninterrupted opportunity to make a cave-system out of the choppers of whose straightness my mother was so proud. She couldn't understand how it was happening. (She probably couldn't understand how so much small change dematerialised from her purse, either.) When a tooth was giving me hell I would try to plug it temporarily by taking a good deep bite into a chocolate bar. Finally there was too much pain to live with and I was introduced, after only token escape attempts, into the surgery of a special dentist for young people, Mr Jolly. He had his chair rigged up as a cowboy saddle with stirrups and you were encouraged to wear toy guns. These latter were supplied by the receptionist if you didn't own any.

With a Ned Kelly cap-pistol holstered low on each hip I felt a bit self-conscious sitting there, not just because I was sixteen years old but because of a dim awareness that my mouth might present an offensive sight to a man whose whole ambience was so radiantly clean. Upon looking into my open maw Mr Jolly reacted only by catching his breath and turning pale. In the first session that was all he did – look around, poke about a bit, and get his nurse to mark up the cavities on a mouth-map – but after it was over I rewarded myself, at the nearest newsagent's, with a Hoadley's Violet Crumble Bar. At the next session a week later he did a bit of drilling, but not much. Such was his method: to proceed slowly and build confidence. He was also very generous with the local anaesthetic. This accorded well with one half of my ambivalent feelings about the hypodermic syringe: on the one hand I demanded to be as desensitised as possible, on the other I hated needles. He overcame my negative tropism by giving a small preliminary injection to dull the impact of the second, larger one. Further injections followed if there was any suspicion of a reawakening tingle from my fat lip. The cumulative effect rendered me numb to the waist. He could have sawn my head off and I wouldn't have felt a thing.

Since my accursed imagination was still alive, and even more terrified of the drill now that I had only its sound from which to deduce what it was doing, he could never step on the accelerator. Any time the noise of the rotating bit rose above a low buzz, I would be arching up out of the chair like a strychnine victim while making, from the back of my throat, the strangled gargles of a turkey choking. These noises had a galvanising effect in the reception area outside, where the waiting children and their anxious mothers erroneously inferred that the current patient had got the drill tangled in his vocal cords.

At that rate there was no hope of filling even one cavity per session. On average it took four trips to plug each hole, with the gap stopped by a temporary filling until the big day came when the cavity could receive its permanent filling of amalgam. Before the amalgam went in, the cavity had first to be lined. The lining included some alcohol-based component which, if it fell on your tongue, burned like Mexican food, but with the mouth jacked open there was nothing to be done except hope the inserted rubber pipe would suck it away along with the spit. Then the amalgam was smeared in, a few flakes at a time, on metal spatulas, like paint from the palette of a slap-happy but somnambulistic Post-Impressionist gradually going mad with the *impasto*. At the subsequent session the hardened filling was polished and the next cavity made its first, tentative encounter with the shy tip of the lethargically turning drill. Since I had something like thirty-four cavities to fill – I can remember for certain that there were more holes than I had teeth – it will be appreciated that the course of treatment stretched over what is called, in Australia, a considerable period of time. Finally all my teeth had been shot full of lead. I had a mouth like two sets of knuckle-dusters. The *pièce de résistance* was fashioned from a nobler metal. It was a heart-shaped gold filling in one of my front teeth. Mr Jolly worked on that one like Benvenuto Cellini on the statue of Perseus. By the time it was in position I had finished high school and was ready to begin university. Mr Jolly told me that of all my unsatisfactory aspects as a patient, the most depressing was the way he couldn't start work on my mouth each week without first cleaning out the debris of chocolate, toffee, liquorice and mashed peanuts from around the very fillings he had spent a good part of his career painstakingly inserting. I got the impression that he wouldn't have minded seeing me take a bit of the pain myself, yet he never succumbed to the temptation. He must have been a saint.

Barry wasn't that but perhaps his straightforwardness was a virtue. Where Mr Jolly would do everything to put fear at rest, Barry would tell you the worst and challenge you to run. 'This next bit's going to hurt like buggery.' He was right every time. Within minutes of each session starting I was making inner vows not to come back next week, but he had a way around that. 'I'm going to leave that molar wide open so the muck inside can dry out, but if you don't come back soon the bludger'll go septic and you'll die in agony.' He did about a year's work in three weeks. Most of my back teeth were beyond hope but the front ones looked like the full allocation unless I laughed, which I didn't feel like doing for some time. The last and hardest job was to clean up my gums. After every few scrapes I flew around the surgery like an open-mouth balloon. The girl from Curl Curl pinned me with a body-slam and the job was done. 'You'd feel a lot less scared,' said Barry, saying goodbye for ever, 'if you understood your real problem.' Wet-eyed with relief, gratitude and remembered pain, I asked him what that was. 'You're a coward.'

10

Fairy Mild Green Liquid Godmother

While having my mouth fixed I had changed residence. Farewell to Tufnell Park. Even through the dull ache in my mouth I could taste the thrill of a new era. Youth was at the helm. London had begun to swing. Films were being made in which it was assumed, almost always erroneously, that the story would be more interesting if the people concerned were to run instead of walk. Nothing could be more up to date than to be a young man with a beard and strange shoes, carrying a suitcase, free-wheeling, on the move. I moved all the way up the road and around the corner, into a loft made available by a nice young married lady who charged a reasonable rent. My pyramid-shaped hutch, which could be entered only via a ladder starting in a top-floor room full of her children, was half the size of the room I had left behind and had even fewer built-in facilities, but by moving two blocks I had entered Kentish Town, so for all practical purposes I was in Hampstead. As part of the same upwardly mobile thrust, I had landed another white-collar job, and this time I wasn't coding reports or filling up charts. I was coding reports *and* filling up charts.

Market Assessment Enterprises had third-floor offices just off High Holborn on the Gamages side of Grays Inn Road. Gamages is gone now and I suppose Market Assessment Enterprises, or MAE, has long been wound up, because it was a happy-go-lucky outfit that was far too much fun to work for. Except for the recently ex-Oxbridge Jeremys and Nigels who owned the company, the work-force consisted exclusively of young fringe-dwellers who worked for no other reason than to finance their intense night life. There were some outstandingly pretty girls, fashionably dressed in high white plastic boots yet always cadging each other's cigarettes. There were young men in sharply cut suits with flared trousers – the first hint of the Carnaby Street look – but they couldn't afford to eat lunch.

The low-paying jobs were in the office, coding the reports. The even-lower-paying jobs were out in the street, where you stood with your report sheet and asked randomly selected people from the passing crowd whether they preferred the cap of the plastic bottle of green liquid detergent fully detachable from the plastic bottle or else attached to the plastic bottle by means of a short plastic attachment. In reality the selection of respondents wasn't random at all, because the only people who would consent to answer such questions were mental defectives or people with such inadequate personalities that any form of conversation came as a blessing. For the first day I tried to be honest but it was hopeless. The only man who gave a coherent set of answers to all twenty-five questions turned out to come from Sweden. Rather than discard the one answer-sheet that made sense, I wrote down that he came from Swindon. It then occurred to me, as it had independently occurred to all my colleagues, that if you could make up the man's address you could also make up the man's answers and even the man himself. The whole thing could be done in the pub.

Employing the same skills which had scored me a perfect mark for my Clinical Case Study in the Sydney University Psychology exams, I produced, at the end of my first week, a set of reports which ensured my promotion to the office staff proper. This meant that I could sit in the office and take the fantasy a step further by coding the incoming reports so that they would be ready for transfer to punched cards. Everyone sat at small desks, as if at school, but talked at the top of his or her voice, as if the school were in the grip of some permanent rag day. The light of spring poured through the windows and illuminated Moira, the girl in the next desk to my right. Moira's physical presence disturbed me in a way that I knew I remembered, but couldn't remember exactly how. Then I suddenly realised that she reminded me of Sonia Humphries, the girl who had sat beside me in the double front-row desk of Class 1B at Kogarah Infants' School in 1946. The resemblance was furthered by Moira's notable deficiency of height. Measured vertically, she lacked inches. Measured around the chest, however, she did not. Moira was the first girl I ever found both attractive and out of proportion. Up to then I had always been drawn towards a classical balance of forces, but Moira made her combination of diminutiveness and excess seem like a romantic challenge. Besides, she was keen – always a potent influence on judgment. Half-way between a garden gnome and one of those country and western singers off whose straining denim shirt-fronts the rhinestones jump like popcorn, she thought I was wonderful and I found it hard not to agree.

Down in the pub – where she regularly paid for her round of drinks after helping me pay for mine – she would sit on the edge of her seat with the toes of her sling-backed shoes just reaching the floor and tell me horror stories about her lover, a company director called Eric. Eric's company, it transpired, dealt principally in goods which had fallen off the back of a van. One of the tell-tale signs of the now efflorescent Sixties was how the much-touted outbreak of classlessness was matched by an obsession with status, so that any fly-by-night operator would call himself a company director merely on the strength of having had his mohair suits made to measure.

Apparently Eric had rescued Moira from her old job as a knife-thrower's assistant in Brighton, but she soon found Eric's idea of looking after her almost as bad as watching the knife-thrower take a stiff drink to steady his hands between the matinee and the main performance. So Moira had run out on Eric and was now covertly occupying an under-eaves bed-sit in Lamb's Conduit Street. While she was telling me this, the evening sunlight flooding through the clear upper panes of the pub windows lit up her beehive of red hair, her freckled face and her chaste white blouse, which didn't seem to drape vertically anywhere except at the back. Just as it was occurring to me that Lamb's Conduit Street wasn't very far away, Moira insisted that I accompany her there immediately. I complied, doing my best to stroll in a casual manner while she trotted beside me. It further occurred to me that all this was too simple. I was right about that, but first there was a short interlude while I enjoyed the uncomplicated delight of a perfectly straight-forward woman. In her little room, decorated only by a chianti-flask lampstand and a suitcase rather like mine, Moira asked for nothing except to give love while having money borrowed from her. She was infinitely exploitable. It should have dawned on me sooner that my predecessors in her favours would be unlikely to let such a bonanza go by default.

What I couldn't hope to guess in advance, however, was the extent and fervour of Moira's gratitude. The mere fact that I did not beat her up was enough to establish me in her mind as a gift from heaven. With desperate urgency she granted me her body as a reward. Amazed to discover that there was someone in whose universe I rated as a kind man, I did my best, through evening after evening, to keep up with her frantic insatia-bility. My landlady grew ever more waspish as I tele-phoned once again to say I would be home very late. Sometimes I arrived home so weary, and so fuddled from the cider with which Moira had kept me primed, that I had trouble climbing the ladder from the children's room up to the loft, and would sit there among the teddy bears until I got my breath back or dawn broke, whichever was the sooner.

The only, but real, trouble with Moira was that there was nothing else she wanted to do. I took her to the NFT to see Chris Marker's *Letter from Siberia*, a documentary film whose exuberantly serious tone of voice still influences everything I do twenty years later. At the time I was knocked sideways. The details of the majestic final sequence are fresh in my mind today. 'There isn't any God, or curses,' said the narrator as the rocket took off, 'only forces – to be overcome.' I didn't agree even then, but I sat transfixed by the rhythm of that voice – the strong view lightly stated. It wasn't words plus pictures. It was words times pictures. At some length I told Moira just how badly the world needed to forget John Grierson and his whole boring tradition. Moira, however, just wanted to get me alone so that she could go on being grateful in the only way she knew. Hazlitt was only half right when he warned his fellow writers that they will dream in vain of the analphabetic woman who will love them for themselves. There is such a woman. What he should have said is that if we find her she will bore us. Moira would have been the ideal concubine if an ideal concubine had been all I wanted. To find out that I wanted something more, or at any rate something else, was disturbing. A fantasy had been made actual and had scared me in the process.

Things got scarier still when I tried taking a night off. The next day at the office Moira was red-eyed from lack of sleep. Just while I was pondering how to disentangle myself from her pneumatic embrace without destroying her newly established faith in mankind, my problem was solved for me. A man walked into the office, stood over her desk, and nodded towards the door. He didn't look quite violent enough to be Company Director Eric but he didn't look like Canon Collins either. She left with him without saying a word. I went after them down the stairs and she must have heard me, because on the last landing before the street I found her facing me. I accused her, with more relief than rancour, of having carried a torch for Eric all along. She told me that the man wasn't Eric. It was the knife-thrower. She was married to him. Then she gave me an uncharacteristically reticent kiss, clattered down the remaining stairs and went out of my life.

I got fired the same day, after a statistical fault in a report about a red plastic tomato-shaped tomato sauce container led to an investigation. The people out in the street had faked their questionnaires as usual, but at least they had built in a few believable discrepancies. For three long and light-headed weeks I had coded the questionnaires while blacking out from the previous night's encounter with Moira. Husbanding my vestigial energies, I had neglected to put in the inconsistencies required by verisimilitude. The result was too perfect, too simple to be believed: rather like Moira herself.

11

The Warping of the Ninth

Failure felt like liberty, so heady was the air. Not only had I to change jobs, I had to change residence as well. Moira had been and gone like Julie Christie in *Sparrows Can't Knack* or *The Loneliness of the Long-Distance Liar*. Another one just like her would be along soon if you waited, and twice as soon if you moved on. All the new films were the same one with a different title: middle-aged entrepreneurs with second houses in up-and-coming Marbella were making money by convincing the young that money didn't matter and the moonlight flit equalled romance.

My landlady, who had probably wanted nothing from me except a sounding board for her justified complaints about her pig of a husband, had not got even that. Instead of bidding me good riddance she put me in the way of a new job and a roof to go with it. An old Oxford chum of hers was starting up, from an address in Chelsea, a prestige publishing house cum second-hand book service. In the first-floor library of his double-knock-through Georgian house I sat to be interviewed, my arms in the sleeves of the Singapore suit held carefully to my sides. He did all the talking. Visions of the future were conjured up: we would be a combination of Bertram Rota and the Officina Bodoni. He would be the management and I would be the staff. Within a short time I would be a company director. Salary would be a matter of agreement from time to time, but I could take it for granted that I would not want for money, make sense? Each of his successive verbal flights was tagged with the rhetorical question 'make sense?', short for 'Does that make sense?' And at that moment it did make sense, although I should have been more worried about the white foam at the corners of his mouth. A no-longer-young semi-titled Englishman is not necessarily suspect just because his complexion is as purple as beetroot and his eyes pop, but if he spits foam without noticing then it is a safe bet that there are other things he isn't noticing either.

His name was Maurice Dillwick. The name Dillwick was famous, not because of him but because of his father, one of those hereditary peers who defy probability not only by donating their services gratis to the public weal but by being rather good at it. The old man had organised shadow factories during the war, organised their demobilisation afterwards, helped nationalise the coal industry, helped rationalise the steel industry, and acted as the kind of benevolent Lord Chamberlain whose civilised tolerance served to perpetuate an inherently stifling institution and thus enfeeble the English theatre for longer than necessary. His was a greatly successful life in all respects but one: his son, though clever, was not quite clever enough to distinguish a passion from a fad or a vocation from a phase. While his father lived, Maurice was kept on short commons, rarely being given more than a few hundred thousand pounds at a time with which to pursue his career as a racing driver, a film director, an explorer or a spy. When the old man hit the soup one day in the House of Lords dining-room, Maurice inherited so much money that not even he was able to lose it all at once, so each new enthusiasm could be pursued until he got tired of it. At the time of my recruitment he had already been a publisher for a year.

Not a lot of publishing had been accomplished in that

time. That was where I would come in: with my fresh approach, uncluttered by stiffly traditional practices, I would give the project a no-nonsense internal structure. In being stimulated to these fantasies about my prowess, Maurice was perhaps aided by two extraneous factors. One was that George Russell had responded to yet another request for a reference, sending, by return air-letter, an encomium which would have sat extravagantly on the shoulders of Pico della Mirandola. (That I ever wasted my professor's time by such demands is of enduring shame to me, and that I should have drained his energies in connection with this particular mare's nest is something I will have to answer for at the last trumpet.) The other document in my favour was a letter from *Encounter*, signed by Stephen Spender himself, accepting my suite of five poems about porpoises. Maurice was almost as impressed by this as I was. He immediately had me cast as the Christopher Brennan of my generation. (From his days as proprietor and editor of *Negozio nero*, an international arts magazine which had cast its net even wider than *Botteghe oscure* but with less accuracy, Maurice had retained an acquaintance with the principal names in the not very long honour roll of Australian literary history.) As a man of letters I would give the new firm – called provisionally Editions Dillwick – not just an internal structure but an antipodean boldness. He appointed me a company director forthwith.

Promoted from staff to management within a week, I still had no cash in hand but was compensated by being given a back room of the house in which to set up my suitcase. My room, like every other room except the second-floor suite in which Maurice slept and dressed, was piled waist-high with stacked books, the stock of a second-hand book dealer whom Maurice had saved from going bust. The second-hand book dealer was an ageing but still sexually active old poet called Willis Cruft who had once, in Alexandria during the war, written apocalyptic verses which Tambimuttu had found bad enough to publish in *Poetry London*. Nowadays Cruft did not ask for much in life except enough cash to drink wine, run a string of Chinese girl-friends and attend the occasional Sibelius concert at the Festival Hall. Maurice having bought his stock from him for an indeterminate sum, Cruft was obliged to wait around in the hope of extracting some petty cash from time to time. Meanwhile, as a company director of Editions Dillwick, he was included in our three-way talks on how the books piled on the floor might be dispatched to the waiting world. His certain knowledge that there could be nothing immediate about this process was tempered by the necessity of not dampening Maurice's enthusiasm. Realism and feigned optimism thus fought an eternal war in his features, which were already deeply cragged by decades of too much wine, too little success and whatever had gone on in Alexandria.

We three directors of Editions Dillwick sat down around a tea-chest full of the standard edition of Bernard Shaw (the red binding, lacking three volumes) to plan the company's future. Maurice called this convocation the Think Tank. Two hours went by while Maurice discarded all our suggestions for the design of the firm's letterhead. More unsettling was that he discarded his own suggestions with equal vehemence. It quickly became apparent that Maurice could not hear an idea without becoming enthusiastic about it, and that he could not become enthusiastic about it without turning against it. What was not yet apparent was that he was like this in large matters as well as in small. But when the builders arrived it all started to become clear, to others if not to me.

Maurice had contracted a building firm called Piranesi Brothers to refurbish the house throughout while the books were still in it. In Maurice, the newly emergent Habitat design ethos had found its ideal lay exponent. He wanted all the old wallpapers out, all the wood stripped and stained, and every plaster surface painted white. The inevitable result was spots of paint-stripper, varnish and white emulsion all over the green New York edition of Henry James (spines of some volumes cracked). Maurice accused the Piranesi Brothers of plotting to work slowly and ruin his stock. The Piranesi Brothers would retire to the first-floor bathroom, barricade themselves in and privately agree that Mr Dillwick was a nutter. Little did they know that Maurice was taping everything they said and compiling a dossier for the future court case. When they drove off in their Dormobile to another job, Maurice would trail them in his green Jensen to find out where they went, then conceal himself and take photographs of them as they hatched plots to spatter Pamastic all over our priceless second editions (endpapers slightly foxed) of the *Complete Poems* of Alice Meynell. It was about this time, acting from an instinct far quicker than lagging thought, that I wrote off to the LCC telling them they would be wise to come through with my Cambridge grant straight away, because I had no other plans and might well become a burden on the social services.

According to Maurice, the Piranesi Brothers were conspiring to cheat him. According to common sense, they were merely, like all small building firms, running several contracts at once in order to turn an honest profit. But common sense had no chance against Maurice's superior intellect. The dossier grew ever fatter. It bulged with photographs, legal documents and transcriptions of taped telephone calls. Finally even Maurice must have begun to notice that he was overwrought, because he gave himself a holiday. 'I'm *bored* with these builders,' he averred, foam much in evidence. 'I have to get away and think about the overall *shape* of the company. I've been pushing myself too *hard* on a day-to-day basis, make sense?' It didn't, because he hadn't, but if that was the way he felt, who was I to argue? Having bought a new

Jensen just like the old one except for a sparkling set of Borrani wire wheels, he disappeared towards the south of France, leaving me in charge.

In charge, that is, of a house full of loose books and frustrated builders. Willis Cruft sensibly declined to consider any advice I might have about how the situation could be retrieved. Correctly diagnosing Editions Dillwick to be an irredeemable folly, he gave himself to Sibelius and the relay of Chinese girls still flying in from Hong Kong. I should have listened to him when he said that things would only get worse on Maurice's return. I preferred, not very passionately, to believe that they would get better. Meanwhile I was in the position of Grand Admiral Dönitz in the few days between Hitler's suicide and the surrender of Germany – I was exercising supreme power over a shambles. To my credit I did not keep up the telephone surveillance on the Piranesi Brothers. My dereliction was in clear breach of Maurice's departing orders, but I would have felt contemptible doing it and anyway I couldn't work the Grundig. To my shame, on the other hand, I went on spending my expense money – there had still been no vulgar talk of salary – instead of handing Maurice my resignation. Handing him my resignation while I was in Chelsea and he in Antibes would not have been easy, but to stay on was taking candy from a baby.

My typical day was spent making tea for the decorators and standing close behind them so I could catch a dollop of varnish before it fell on the cover of *The Apes of God* (reprint, two signatures out of order, otherwise fair) and halved its already negligible value. In the evenings I wooed an Australian girl called Robin who had a marvellous clear skin and was teetering on the verge of deciding not to be a strict Catholic. To encourage her in that direction I took her to see every Buñuel movie in town. When *Los Olvidados* was on at the Chelsea Arts cinema I took her there two nights running but still couldn't slide my hand between her breasts without getting my wrist tangled in the chain of her crucifix. My large talk about being a director and chief executive of Editions Dillwick didn't work the trick either. The letter from the LCC which I had hoped would excuse me two years of waiting for Cambridge only excused me one year. My determination was plain, they said, but it would have to wait until the October after next to attain its object. This was a disappointment. Another letter capped disappointment with disaster: Stephen Spender wrote to say that the number of poems accepted for *Encounter* was now so great that he could see no prospect of printing mine in the foreseeable future. He could, however, arrange to have them published immediately in another magazine, whose name, if I remember correctly, was *Periphery*, or perhaps *Margin*. I wrote back to say that I preferred the original arrangement, which I regarded as a promise, and that the unforeseeable future would do me fine. Perhaps my language was too forceful, because I received no reply. The word 'galah' is an acceptable term of mild remonstrance among Australians. The English, not knowing what a galah is, tend to take offence.

Downcast, I forgot to be the anti-Catholic polemicist and company director. My real self, such as it was, showed through. Robin must have decided either that she liked it or that she might like it after a few things had been done to it, because she hung her scalloped-edged white slip over the back of a chair and took me to bed. Or rather, I took her to bed, the bed being mine: there were books stacked all around it and I spent a lot of time reassembling the collected works of Hugh Walpole after Robin fell over them on her way back from the bathroom in the dark. She looked marvellous dressed in a towel and a crucifix. It made me feel like the hero in one of those *Nouvelle vague* films that were coming out just about then. I lay back like Jean-Paul Pierre or Pierre-Jean Paul or whatever the twerp's name was, the sheet tucked around my waist and a cigarette dangling dangerously from my lower lip.

Very dangerously, as it turned out. The damage to the sheet was extensive and I could easily have burned Robin to death. There was worse. Availing myself of Maurice's stereo, I had been listening half a dozen times a day to his two-disc set of Beethoven's Ninth conducted by Toscanini. The adagio, in particular, sent me into a trance. What delicacy, and yet what drive! How little rubato and yet how supple! It was in just such a mesmer-ised condition that I left the two records on top of the switched-on amplifier while I took Robin to the pub, there to help her overcome her inhibitions about drinking by showing her what an entertaining fellow I became when inebriated. Having helped me home, Robin was the first to notice that the Toscanini records had acquired crinkled edges. As well as making me feel iller – iller, that is, than how ill I felt from the whiff of molten vinyl, as well as how ill I was already feeling anyway – their patent unplayability made me feel inadequate. Doubtless Maurice had too many toys: but I was in a position of trust. 'Position of truss,' I explained tearfully to Robin. Late that night, without her knowledge, I zig-zagged down the corridor through the cairns of books and trans-ferred the warped discs from the top of a stack of albums to the bottom, partly from the slim conviction that the weight would flatten them out, mainly in the pious hope that Maurice would never twig. After all, he had so much stuff.

Robin understood when I told her that I had to go to Italy. Françoise, the girl I had left behind in Australia, was now studying in Florence and could no doubt arrange accommodation while I spent a week recuperating from vinyl poisoning. I could tell that Robin understood be-cause she didn't physically oppose my going, and in those days I construed absence of explicit opposition as a whole-hearted endorsement. I was careful to borrow some spending money as additional evidence of her goodwill. The petty cash left behind by Maurice would cover the plane ticket, and I planned to hitchhike after I got to Milan. But there would be cigarettes to buy. Robin was the first to appreciate that a New Wave hero must have his cigarettes, which in Italy, I had heard, were hard to obtain. In my jeans, T-shirt, combat jacket, beard and dangling cigarette I reckoned I looked the sort of tough customer the Italians would take seriously. To complete the ensemble I had a bang-up-to-date pair of new shoes. Black winklepickers so long in the toe that the distance from the front of my foot to the front of the shoe was greater than to the heel, they looked dazzling down there. Even while staring straight ahead I could see the toes of my shoes in my peripheral vision. Equipped to kick the brains out of a fly, I had to walk with my feet slightly sideways, like a ballet dancer. Somehow I reached Gatwick, boarded a Dan-Air DC7-C charter flight, and headed for that far-off country the British call Europe.

12

Fiorenza, Fiorenza

Everything went fine until Milan, because the pilot was making all the hard decisions. After that I was on my own. Immediately people started behaving very strangely. I had already attracted a few sideways glances from some of the Italians on the plane, but here in the actual Italy the Italians stared openly. They formed groups so as to co-ordinate their unblinking scrutiny. At first I thought it was the shoes, but the immigration official couldn't see them from inside his glass booth, and he stared too. Did I bear a startling resemblance to the lost king Vittorio Emmanuele IV? Not too fanciful a notion, because it rapidly became apparent that the focus of interest was the beard. I had the only beard in Italy. (No kidding: the first modern native Italian beards were grown after the Florence floods, still some time in the future.) As I her-ringboned along in my winklepickers with my beard collecting dust, I must have struck the locals as a failed cross-country skier making fun of Garibaldi.

Another drawback was that nobody spoke English. As I was later to learn, you need only ten words of their language and the Italians will gladly help you with the rest, but at that stage I had only three words and a punctuation mark: '*Autostrada del Sole*?' I was looking for the Highway of the Sun. When I said this phrase with an interrogative inflection while doing my gestural imitation of a six-lane highway, people crossed themselves. Some of them crossed the street. But a few brave souls pointed the way, so that after about two hours of doing my frog-man walk through the killing midday heat I had reached the highway at a spot where it looked like I might get a lift, if one of the hurtling cars would only stop. After another two hours one did. It had an English driver: a Unilever accountant who said he could take me as far as Piacenza. While I drank two bottles of orangeade out of a six-pack and the entire contents of a flask of mineral water, he explained that it wasn't just the beard which kept me rooted to the hard shoulder, it was also that hitchhiking was forbidden. Dimly I remembered Françoise having told me that in her last letter. Receiving advice, ignoring it, and then later finding out the hard way how good it was, has been the story of my life. One of these days the Good Samaritan might fail to materialise, or might not have any orangeade with him when he does.

Just outside the Piacenza exit my saviour set me off at a point where I might conceivably pick up another lift south, but he warned me not to bank on it. After an hour and a half of watching Fiats, Lancias and Alfas go by both ways like an exchange of bullets, I got the point and started walking towards town. It was a long way and I was grateful when a three-ton truck heading in that direction slowed down and stopped just ahead. The old hooked thumb had worked at last. When the driver leaned out, he doubled my relief by speaking English.

'You want a lift?'

'Yes, actually.'

'Yes, actually. You from England?'

'Australia.'

'Australia. I hear your accent now. I was in Australia, at the Snowy River Project. I do not like Australians. Here in Italy we do not like the beard. I drive into town, get some of my friends, we come back and fix you good.'

On the other side of the roadside ditch there were cabbages growing among which I hid, but after about another hour it started looking probable that he would not come back, so I began walking again, this time without the extended thumb. The land smelled like piss but that could have been the way I felt. Having to turn my feet sideways even to limp successfully, I had a terrific pain in the ankle, so by the time I got to Piacenza railway station I had barely enough strength left to get my wallet out. Spending all my remaining money on a ticket to Florence was rendered needlessly complicated by the fact that none of the ticket-sellers had ever heard of the place. At last their supervisor showed up and set them straight by informing them that the city they had always referred to as 'Firenze' was in reality called Florence. It took a long time to sort out and I missed a train while it was happening, but the next train had a name – *accelerato* – that sounded fast enough to make up the difference.

It transpired that *accelerato* was the Italian word for 'stopping at every station and going very slowly in between so as not to overshoot'. I arrived at Florence long after dark and reached Françoise's *pensione* near the Medici Palace long after that, having frequently lost my way through being obliged to turn around and disperse the crowd following my beard. The landlady took one look at me and immediately appointed herself Françoise's guardian. I was allowed into Françoise's cool, terracotta-tile-floored room long enough to wash the dust from my face, but the landlady stood in the doorway with her powerful arms folded and large chin raised high, thereby abetting an already remarkable physical resemblance to Mussolini. I ended up sleeping on the floor of a partitioned-off section of a decrepit palace down behind the Piazza della Signoria. The owner of the flat, a spotty but sweet girl called Barbara, was an old school friend of Françoise's from Australia. I don't owe Barbara any money – Françoise paid the rent – but I owe her a lot for her time and concern, and it worries me now that I didn't realise that then. When I met her again in London the following year, I was short with her, instead of taking the trouble to hark fondly back as she expected. Eventually too many such incidents rankled enough to make me change my ways – to the extent, anyway, of never taking any favours that I would not have time to be grateful for. It sounds like a cold man's rule and I'm afraid it is, but I was even worse before I thought of it.

My ill-judged arrival had put Françoise in a false position. Nowadays you have to go pretty far south in Italy before you encounter the widespread belief that any foreign girl is a whore unless her father and two brothers drive her around in an armoured car. In those days the whole of Italy was like that. Françoise, clearly a well brought-up girl, had been highly thought of in the *pensione* and therefore subject only to the usual relentless innuendo from the male guests, actual attempts at molestation and rape being confined to the street, down which, since she did not look notably foreign, she walked at the same hazard as any other presentable woman – i.e., young male pests, known locally as *pappagalli*, followed her in cat-calling groups, while older male pests appeared suddenly out of doorways or lunged from cars in order to run a lightly touching hand over her bottom and whisper obscenities in her ear. Though all this was standard stuff to which she was well accustomed, I would shout with anger when I saw it happen. I should have been angry with myself, because it was my advent which had ensured that the *pensione* was no longer her refuge. Françoise was now known to keep open company with a young man not her husband. Moreover, he had a beard, unacceptable shoes and shouted a great deal. The landlady, by dint of a long speech delivered in front of the assembled guests during which she profiled in true *il Duce* style with her chin as high as her forehead while they

burst into spontaneous applause, made it clear to Fran-
çoise that I was to be met outside if at all.

To shave off the beard would have reduced the city-
wide brouhaha to more manageable proportions, but my
dander was up. We radical socialists could always be
relied upon to take a stand when there was no hope of
budging the status quo and every chance of embarrassing
our friends. Françoise would have been well justified in
washing her hands of me but she was a born educator.
Angry, unbalanced and flailing as I was, I still found the
great city opening up before me. She knew just where to
take me. In the Uffizi I was stood in front of the Giotto
madonna, the Portinari altarpiece by van der Goes, the
Leonardo Annunciation and the two wide-screen Botti-
cellis. In the Bargello I met Michelangelo's Brutus face
to face. (He was on the first floor in those days: they put
him downstairs after the flood.) To the Accademia for
Michelangelo's slaves and to the Medici chapel for his
times of day. Across the river to the Brancacci chapel,
where I pretended to see, and perhaps already saw, the
difference when Masaccio took over the job of painting
the walls. It was Orientation Week all over again: the
edited highlights, at which I still might have gagged
unless wisely led. But Françoise was a real teacher and
for once I was a serious student. It was a serious city.
The surf of forgotten faces in the Gozzoli and Ghirlandaio
frescoes I might conceivably have laughed off. Michel-
angelo's *terribilità*, when it transfixed me through the
stone eyes of Brutus, shook the soul. It was so like being
looked at by Françoise's landlady.

My self-esteem took a battering. Part of being over-
whelmed by a big new subject is the shame of realising
that you knew nothing about it before. Helping me to feel
worse were the twin facts that I ended up alone on
Barbara's floor every night, and that whenever Françoise
took me to meet her friends it rapidly turned out that
everybody wanted to speak Italian except me. Or, rather,

including me, except that I didn't know how. Up until that time I had been pleased, not to say proud, to remain monolingual. Now came the climb-down. I can even remember the moment. It was at an early-evening drinks party on a grassy little hill behind a big house on the other side of the Arno. The men had their sleeves rolled up in the heat and the women were bare-shouldered in cool silk dresses and high-heeled sandals. Françoise and her friend Gabriella were arguing with Franco, an economics lecturer at Florence University and notable contributor to the kind of film magazine, just then becoming prominent, edited by Bellocchio's cousin or Bertolucci's brother. Franco had reacted against Wölflinn's line on the *cinquecento* to the extent of proclaiming Andrea del Sarto no good at all, whereas the women thought that the cartoons in the Chiostro della Scala were rather marvellous. I had my own, perhaps half-baked, opinions on this matter, but by the time I had persuaded Françoise to translate them, the conversation had moved on to the merits of Fellini, with specific reference to *Otto e mezzo*. Franco thought the film a fraud. Gabriella disagreed. Françoise strongly disagreed, as well she might, because we had seen the film together the previous evening, she for the second time and I for the third, although it had been my first time without the aid of subtitles. I disagreed so strongly that I took Françoise aside, not really hurting her arm that much, and urgently briefed her on my position. When we turned back to the conversation, Franco and Gabriella were yelling at each other simultaneously, but I forced Françoise to interrupt them and advance my argument. They greeted it with raised eyebrows and embarrassed shiftings from foot to foot. It was because of the irrelevance of Fellini's transcendental imagination to the question of who might succeed Palmiro Togliatti as leader of the Communist Party.

Experiencing inarticulacy for the first time since the

cradle, I was so frustrated that I dug the toes of my winklepickers into the hill and stood there bouncing with unexploded energy, like a woodchopper on his plank waiting for a signal that never came. That same night, Françoise sat down beside me with a volume of Dante and construed a few lines of the *Inferno* to begin showing me how the language worked. *Per me si va tra la perduta gente.* Through me you go among the lost people. A line that crushed the heart, but in the middle of it you could say *tra la.* It was music.

Thus it was, when I reached Milan on the return journey and was unable to pay the airport tax because of having bought too many cigarettes at the railway station, that I was able, out of my ten-word vocabulary, to come up with the one word required: *Disastro!* I said it repeatedly with much wringing of hands, until an Indian passenger booked on my flight gave me 1,000 lire and waved aside all talk of repayment. I have liked Indians ever since. The alternative would have been to cast myself on the mercy of the Italian airport police, who all looked as if they were closely related to a certain truck-driver in Piacenza.

Back in London, my problems had not gone away. Indeed while I had been away they had joined forces. Robin was cheesed off with me for some reason; Willis Cruft was accusing me of having cut him off from the petty cash; the builders had not only given up but taken to using the back garden as a storehouse for spare equipment; and Maurice's mother was on the premises to inform me that I must leave for Glyndebourne immediately. Rapidly adapting Maurice's dinner jacket to my differently arranged proportions, the grey-haired but energetic Lady Dillwick had her mouth full of pins half the time, but she spent the other half telling me that since Maurice had arranged to take a party to see *Capriccio* and then decided that he would rather go off to the Côte d'Azur instead, it was up to his substitute to fill in.

Lady Dillwick's decisiveness was aided by her technique of not letting anyone else finish a sentence. This habit was later to be made familiar by Britain's first woman Prime Minister, but at the time it was a new one on me. As I stood there in my underpants while Lady Dillwick took up her son's satin-piped black trousers by about six inches, I did my best to disqualify myself for the task. 'I'm not even sure where Gly . . . ' 'Maurice ought to realise that I've better things to do with my *time* than get him out of these messes.' 'How will I know wh . . . ' 'Those pointed shoes won't be suitable at all.'

Maurice's patent leather pumps were three sizes too big for me so Lady Dillwick padded them with Kleenex. Trepidatiously setting off, I reached the taxi before the heels of the shoes left the house. Lady Dillwick waved me away with an air of 'There, that's *that* taken care of.' I had begun to get an inkling of why Maurice was the way he was. At Victoria I met my companions for the venture. They were a bald, decrepit avant-garde publisher, his beautiful but plastered interior decorator wife, and his large, ageing, Central American senior editor, a woman who eked out an Elizabeth Bergner voice by wearing wooden jewellery and an ankle-length fur coat – rarely a wise idea in summer, even if the summer is English. On top of daring to import such marginal American writers as Alexander Lobrau (*The Beatified Deserters*) and Brad Krocus (*Absorbent Gauze Swabs* and *Violators Turned Away*), the publisher was currently notorious for staging the first of those Happenings by which London was now establishing its pioneering position of being only just behind New York. I had read about how he had invited fashionable society to a dark room off Shaftesbury Avenue full of actors pretending to be tramps and drunks, through which noisomely struggling mass the perfumed invitees had to find their way while the air filled with finely sprayed water and taped traffic noise. The assembled notables all agreed that this experience was somehow radically and liberatingly different from everyday life in the street outside. Unfortunately the publisher, who like so many promoters of the youth craze was in a state of advanced middle age compounded by bibulous excess, had got the idea that in an ideal world all the Happenings would join together with no intervening periods of the quotidian. He now had the brainwave, for example, of getting down to Glyndebourne without any of us purchasing a train ticket. If you did, you were a spoilsport. I'm sorry to say that I was craven enough to go along with this, instead of doing what I should have done, namely spoiling the sport. When we got off the train it turned out that we had to cheat on the bus too, with each of us pretending that someone else was paying. I was still blushing with shame and fear half-way through the first act of the opera. Then I started paying attention to one of the most hypnotic sounds I had heard in my life. It was the sound of the Central American senior editor, massive in the seat beside me, telling her string of wooden beads like a rosary.

During the picnic dinner at interval my companions all had the chance to have a good laugh about how the emergency stitching in my trousers had started to come adrift. I did my best to divert their attention by explaining that this whole den of privilege and ridiculously attenuated pastiche would be enough reason in itself to start a socialist revolution forthwith. My fervour masked awkwardness. What with the difficulty I was experiencing in keeping my shoes on and my trousers from unfurling like the inadequately reefed sails of a pirate ship with a drunken crew, I had begun to feel a bit self-conscious. But most of the other men present were reassuringly scruffy. Here was my first lesson on the resolutely maintained untidiness and ill-health of the English upper orders. In baggy evening dress and old before their time, they displayed gapped and tangled teeth in loosely open mouths. Gently shedding dandruff, they lurched across the lawn. When they stood at the bar they looked like Lee Trevino putting. Here also would have been my first lesson in opera, but I found the piece too tenuous to grasp except for the Countess's long soliloquy, during which even the senior editor was charmed into interrupting her death-rattle. Doubtless the way Elisabeth Söderström looked was a help to me in focusing on how she sounded, but I would probably have been captured even had she been less graceful. For a few minutes I got a glimpse into an unsuspected realm of lyrical subtlety. Then the brusque rattling of the wooden beads began again.

Back to Victoria we scaled, one of my trouser legs now forming a black concertina above its canoe-like shoe. That was the night I should have packed it in: random pin money and inappropriate pay-offs did not add up to a salary, and keeping paint-spots off stacked books was the work of a scarecrow. Instead I stuck around. Robin, whose frown of welcome had soon melted into resignation, was there most evenings to cook a meal and help me move the heavier items of builders' equipment. It was a place to live; it was the sort of sinecure, I told myself, that artists had always taken with a clear conscience; and it was certain that Maurice, when he got back, would be better or at least no worse. So I let another three weeks of lightly disguised idleness go by. Luckily for appearances, if not for my conscience, I was actually hard at work transferring an unsaleable almost complete edition of John Galsworthy out of the way of the plasterers when Maurice's Jensen announced its arrival outside by ramming the builders' skip with its left headlight. Tanned the colour of butterscotch and still wearing his Côte d'Azur walking-out dress of rope-soled canvas shoes, lightweight seersucker slacks and a pale-blue T-shirt with a little white anchor, Maurice came bounding up the steps to announce that the positioning of the skip was evidence incontrovertibly establishing the conspiracy between the Piranesi Brothers and the team of Russian spies which MI5 had asked him to keep tabs on in Cannes.

Apparently that was why he had been gone so long. From his unobtrusive vantage point at a table beside the swimming pool in front of the Majestic, he had been surreptitiously photographing the Russian film delegates as they took their constitutional along the Croisette each morning, make sense? Then it had emerged, in response to discreet enquiries, that a beautiful woman called Valentina Pirenucci was booked into the same hotel as the Russians. As Maurice excitedly began telling me about the love affair that he had almost had with her – he was being set up, he could see that now – he pushed a cigarette through the screen of foam joining his lips and lit it more than half-way down, almost at the filter. He looked accusingly at the flaming ruins of the cigarette. Then he looked accusingly at me. He wanted to know what I had accomplished. Apart from getting to Glynde-bourne and back alive while dressed as Groucho Marx, I had accomplished nothing, so there was not a lot I could say. He looked at me as if I was part of the conspiracy. He was right. I was. Anyone who did any kind of business at all with Maurice was only helping him further into confusion. The decent thing to do was to get out straight away, and I had not done it. Now, too late, I tried to make up for my opportunism. But I had still not finished packing my bag that night when I heard, drifting along the corridor from Maurice's locked bedroom, the sound, horribly distorted, of the adagio of Beethoven's Ninth Symphony, conducted by Toscanini. Maurice had discovered the final piece of evidence. It all made sense.

13

Like a Burnished Throne

Charlie came to my rescue, unfortunately. In that great age of the company director, Charlie was the company director epitomised. He had a one-man import-export business. He could get things for you. If you had things you didn't want, he could take them away. Around the Chelsea pubs he was a conspicuous figure, not just because of a major squint but because of his promiscuous taste in fast foreign cars. Peter Sellers had a new car every week but Charlie had a new one every day. On Monday it was a Maserati with a body by Touring of Milan and on Tuesday it was a Mercedes-Benz 300SL with gull-wing doors. None of the cars really worked, but he didn't own them long enough for them to stop working entirely. They stopped working entirely for the people he sold them to. While he was driving them, they went, just. 'Hop in,' Charlie would say from an out-of-date yet eternally beautiful Zagato-bodied 2+2 Ferrari. After you had hopped in, you would wonder why the car was going so slowly. You couldn't wonder it aloud because of the noise kicked up by the chain-driven overhead camshafts. At the next pub, Charlie would explain convincingly how everything would be all right tomorrow, once the drip-feed venturi to the rocker-boxes had been greased. 'Fancy another jar? Your round.'

Charlie said I could live on one of his boats: the one

moored at Twickenham. The rent sounded stiff but he reassured me by saying that the boat was an ocean-going job. 'None of your put-put boats what fart about on a river.' As we headed west in an off-white Lancia Aprilia drop-head with my suitcase in the back, I had visions of a modest but comfortable state-room on the sort of yacht that would not be ashamed of itself if anchored in the lee of Niarchos or Onassis. And indeed *The Relief of Mafeking* was the biggest thing in the basin, but only because it was a coal barge. An ocean-goer in the sense that it had long ago made regular trips to and from Newcastle by sea rather than canal, my new home was so broad in the beam that it was practically circular. Charlie soon had me convinced that this was an advantage. 'Your so-called sleek lines can't give you this, mate,' he said with an expansive gesture in the living space between decks. 'What you've got here is width.' As we stood there with our heads bowed, I had to agree that there was width. What there wasn't was height, but I failed to remark this, being too excited by the prospect of the well-joined planks below and above. I hardly needed Charlie to tell me that there was no workmanship like that nowadays. He showed me how the Calor gas cooking ring worked, warned me that the toilet might be a bit tricky, and left me to unpack. Standing on deck to wave goodbye, I felt like Horatio Hornblower on the bridge of his first command. Lesser boats crowded the basin, in which the tide was so low that some of the water was hard to distinguish from mud. Presumably the smell would be less piercing when the water rose, and meanwhile the Lancia was a reassuring sight as it roared away, stopping only once while Charlie lifted the bonnet to tinker with the engine.

Flushing the toilet was no problem as long as the tide remained out. All you had to do was kick the foot-crank twenty or thirty times until with a loud *kerchunga* the bowl emptied into the bilges. When the tide came in, however,

I was saddened to discover that the same process emptied the bilges into the bowl. By that time it was late at night and it had started to rain. The drumming of the rain on the deck was at first a comfort. But after a not very long time there was the less snug sound of the rain that was coming through the deck and dropping on my floor. It happened only where the fine workmanship of the planks was no longer reinforced by caulking. One such place was in the exact centre of the cabin, so that the puddle formed at the apex of the curved floor and distributed itself very evenly in all directions. A carefully positioned bucket could only delay this process, and anyway I didn't have one. So I went on deck in the driving rain, got down on my knees and found the hole. An old piece of canvas stretched across would soon fix that. There were no old pieces of canvas. I laid out one of my tea-coloured nylon drip-dry shirts and weighed it down around the edges with some bits of wood whose nautical name echoed vaguely in the memory. Belittling pins? Bollocks? The whole operation took no more than twenty minutes, so I didn't really get that much wetter than I would have if I had stood in the centre of my cabin all night directly under the leak.

Next morning another drawback revealed itself. My new home was a long way from the centre of London. Unless Charlie turned up on some errand or other I would have to go in by train or Green Line bus. For a few days I waited for Charlie but it was becoming imperative to find a job, so finally I spent a whole morning getting to town and putting my name down to be considered by London Transport for a job on the tube. They were looking for guards, not drivers. This suited me. I couldn't drive a car but thought that I could probably guard a train, and perhaps work on the odd poem between stations. I could see myself being cheery, useful, a good man in a crisis. Trollope had designed the pillar-box. Keats, Chekhov and Schnitzler had all been doctors.

T. S. Eliot had worked in a bank and Wallace Stevens for an insurance company. I would be a tube guard. Obviously I would be overqualified but I was willing to forget about that in return for a steady income and travel privileges – these latter being particularly welcome to someone living a long way away by water on a ship that could not sail. The next day, in the Singapore suit and the winklepickers, the beard trimmed with nail scissors, I sat down, with almost a hundred other candidates, for the intelligence test. Judiciously I soft-pedalled the brainy stuff, neglecting to mention my degree and doing my best to keep Schopenhauer's name out of it. I must have done all right because after half an hour's wait I was sent into another room for the psychological test. This time there were only about fifty candidates. The examiner sat at a desk. You were signalled forward to occupy the seat opposite him when the previous occupant had been dismissed, after a greater or shorter time. Obviously the long interviews were the more successful ones. Some of the interviews were as short as five minutes. Mine was the only one that lasted a minute and a half. I can remember the questions now. 'Why did you leave your last job?' 'Why did you leave the job before that?' 'And the one before that?' I can't recall my answers, except that they were short at first and grew progressively shorter. His closing statement, I thought, revealed a lack of sensitivity which helped to explain why, as a psychologist, he had risen no higher than the underground railway. 'You have failed the psychological test and we are unable to offer you a position.'

Failing to get down that hole was my low point. Or so I thought, assuming that the task was easy. Actually such jobs – being a postman is another one I still covet – demand exactly the sort of elementary yet responsible alertness that the congenital dreamer is least qualified to give. There is a consoling passage in *Dichtung und Wahrheit* about our capabilities being forecast by our dreams, although it might just mean that Goethe would have made a lousy tube guard. But I was still far short of a full self-appraisal. I was also short of cash. Robin, who worked in a Baker Street bookshop, trekked out to Twickenham often enough to keep me from dying of malnutrition, but the fares and the food used up a disheartening proportion – disheartening even for me, let alone for her – of whatever was left over from keeping herself alive. Where was Charlie?

He arrived one morning at the wheel of a Lagonda, handed me a parallel text of *Les Fleurs du mal*, and told me to bring my toothbrush because we were going to Paris. If I helped him load some furniture into his van in London and unload it in the Flea Market in Paris, there would be something in it for me and I would see the City of Light. The noise of the Lagonda drowned the actual mention of how much the something was. Lagondas were not supposed to be noisy. This one had gear-box trouble. But the van, to which we transferred at Charlie's lock-up garage in Fulham, worked well enough. It was a little blue Bedford tailgate number whose rear tray we carefully filled with solid English furniture – old rosewood military chests and stuff like that. When we reached Dover, I was impressed but not surprised to hear Charlie tell the British customs men that the gear, all French originally, had belonged to his French-born great-aunt, long resident in England, who had recently died tragically of cancer, of the rectum in point of fact, so that the residue of her worldly goods was now returning to her bereaved half-sister in Auteuil. While this was being said I sat there reading Baudelaire as instructed, no doubt to give the impression of being part of the household. At Calais, Charlie told the French customs men that the stuff was all English, of negligible value as you could tell from the chipped inlays, and that it was on its way to furnish the flat of the eccentric new Paris bureau chief of the *Financial Times*. Behold his artistically gifted son, soon to be studying French literature at the Sorbonne. Charlie got most of this across with gestures but there was quite a bit of French mixed in. I was so dumbfounded that I must have looked artistically gifted, because the *douaniers* waved us through. Since the furniture plainly *was* English, and therefore not part of *le patrimoine*, perhaps they didn't care whether Charlie was profiteering or not. Anyhow, we were soon bowling happily down the *route nationale*, with the poplars strobing away on each side.

Under a bright sun we made good time but it was a bit bumpy. Some of the lashings in the back came unstuck so I was standing up there to keep a chest of drawers and a cupboard from knocking into each other when Charlie tooted the horn and I looked ahead and saw Paris. The city lay low among the hills like a dry lake of violet talcum with a little pistachio model of the Eiffel Tower sticking up. It was the Eiffel Tower. Delirium at first glance.

At the Flea Market our consignment of furniture sold out straight away. Charlie handed me my commission: a wad of jokey paper napkins with coloured pictures of people like Richelieu and Mazarin. The wise move would have been to hand the money straight back to him and thus clear up what I would soon owe for rent, but instead I toured the open-air bookstalls along the banks of the Seine, bending over the green-painted bins like a starving parrot over a box of seeds. Books in French scarcely counted as a wise purchase, since I couldn't read more than the odd word of them, but I was working on the assumption that one day I would be able to. Charlie had friends in Paris with whom we had dinner. I didn't enjoy it much because they spoke little English and looked as if they had been left out of a crime movie starring Jean Gabin because they were too sinister. This especially applied to the women. Charlie's *mauvais garçon* squint fitted right in. The rest of him fitted in too: he spoke the international language of where to get things. I couldn't keep up. But the wine I handled quite well, needing, when I bunked down on somebody's floor, scarcely any help to undress. A less clouded happiness came next morning, when I sat outside a café at the crossroads of the Boulevard Saint-Michel and the Boulevard Saint-Germain, drank cognac and watched the girls on their way to work. I had never seen so much prettiness all in the one place. Charlie explained how they did it, with their small wages all going on clothes and nowhere to live except a cold-water broom cupboard. 'Your actual Frog bird,' he announced, 'has got eyes of her own.' Though my own eyes were as yet untrained, I could see straight away that the silk-and-cotton-clad shop assistant clicking along on her way to the Galeries Lafayette was an entirely different proposition from her London counterpart, teetering towards C & A in a black-lacquered hair helmet, cadaverous white face-mask, laddered tights and a skirt no bigger than her belt. It was the difference between *chic* and shock. Calling myself studious, I ogled unashamed, until Charlie said it was time to go.

Zonked by the cognac I slept all the way to London. At Fulham, Charlie climbed into the Lagonda and went somewhere else, so with his strong hints about the desirability of a prompt rent settlement still echoing in my ears I got back to the barge by Green Line bus in time to discover how the deck looked after the tide had gone far enough out to prove the theory – common among the basin's regular inhabitants, I now learned – that *The Relief of Mafeking* had been incorrectly moored. The tide was back in again but a lot of the caulking on deck had gone missing from between the planks. I found some of it in my cabin. My bed, which had been a mattress with a blanket on it, was now a mattress with a blanket and bits of tar on it. Luckily they were too old to be still sticky.

Paying a return visit as arranged, Françoise arrived at Gatwick and with her usual cool head found her way, against all the odds, to my floating palace. I would have met her at the airport, but for some reason Robin wouldn't lend me the money. The tide was out and the yacht basin wasn't looking its best. There was something particularly depressing about how the brown milk bottles sticking up out of the mud were full of water. Standing at the foot of the gangway, Françoise looked out of place in her blue silk blouse, pale-grey straight skirt and hand-made high-heeled suede sandals. She had always had the gift of bringing order and elegance to her surroundings. This new challenge, her expression suggested, might be beyond her. Showing her down to my quarters, I made a nervous joke about Pandora and the Flying Dutchman, before remembering that Pandora was the wrong name to mention. So I switched the frame of reference to Cleopatra's barge.

It didn't rain, so at least we didn't get wet. But without rain there was no relief from the heat. The tide came in and did something to tame the smell, but it did nothing for the toilet, which turned out to be the final insult. In a few days Françoise did a lot to make the place habitable and my intake of foodstuffs less toxic. I was eating salads and there was a pillowcase on the pillow. But a toilet that worked in reverse was too much. Until it should be time for her charter flight back to Italy, she went to stay with the girls in Melbury Road.

Gallantly I carried her suitcase. There was a party going on when we arrived. Robin was there, looking a bit distant for some reason. Françoise didn't look very tolerant either so I danced with a tall girl called Joanne who had recently got off the boat. I told her that I had recently got off a boat too. Just when I had got her laughing at the story about the blow-back toilet her boyfriend moved in on her, so I found myself talking to an old acquaintance from Sydney called Nick Thesinger. At Sydney University Nick had been the star actor of his final year just as I was starting off as a freshman. He had left for England with the high hopes of his friends filling his sails, although he himself had always been realistic enough to guess that London needed Australian actors the way Newcastle upon Tyne needed coal from Newcastle, NSW. So it had proved, and within a year he had been forced into supply-teaching, to eke out what he called 'a small competence' of money from home. But schoolteaching had soon become more than just a living. 'At Stratford, I'd be lucky to carry a spear a year,' he explained. 'At the dear old school I'm simply *forced* to play Macbeth, Hotspur and Richard III every morning, with Hamlet for lunch and Lear in the afternoon. One's thespian urges aren't just satisfied, darling. The relevant glands are *squeezed dry*.' His teacher's salary plus the small competence enabled him to keep a set of rooms just off Baker Street. He had a spare bedroom, into which I was invited to move as soon as was practicable. As to rent, the sum mentioned was more than I had, yet so would have been any other sum no matter how small, because next morning everything I had left went on getting back to the barge and leaving a token pay-off for Charlie. You couldn't really have called it a midnight flit. For one thing, it was daylight. For another, the rent I owed him was more than offset, in my opinion, by the psychic and perhaps physical damage inflicted by the leaking ceiling and the retrodynamic dunny. I drew up a sort of account sheet explaining all this, weighed it down with a few coins, packed my bag and headed down the gang-plank towards the Green Line bus stop, watched by a large woman with piled-up ginger hair who was sunbathing in bursting bra and colossal pink satin bloomers on the deck of a small launch which at first appeared to be listing under her weight, but which on closer examination proved to be stuck in the mud with one side propped up by the rust-eaten remains of a wrought-iron bedstead. The nautical phase of my life was over.

The musical phase now began. Like Françoise a born

teacher, Nick was one of those opera fanatics with the gift of putting you on rather than off. In Australia I had discovered jazz because nobody at Sydney University could very well escape it. Classical music had come to me later and piecemeal. On swimming parties to Avalon with the Bellevue Hill mob at weekends, I had acquired their taste for such stirring stuff as Haydn's trumpet concerto and Beethoven's Seventh. In London I had become intimate with Beethoven's Ninth in the manner already related. More happily, Joyce Grenfell had taken me to the Festival Hall to see the Borodin Quartet play Beethoven's late quartets and Klemperer conduct Bach's Brandenburg concertos. I say 'see' rather than 'hear' because I couldn't take my eyes off the Borodin cellist's tapping foot or Klemperer's right index finger, especially the latter. As the old master sat there in his wheelchair, it was the only part of him that could still move.

But these were scattered experiences and no trained voice had been involved save Söderström's in *Capriccio*, heard intermittently through the machine-gun beads of my companion at Glyndebourne. Nick gave me an immersion course, starting with two scenes in *Der Rosenkavalier*: the Presentation of the Silver Rose and the last act trio. From the first day of this exposure, the bathroom rang to my imitation of Sena Jurinac, Elisabeth Schwarzkopf and Teresa Stich Randall. Lacking the vocal equipment to impersonate any of these women singly, I compromised by providing a vigorous pastiche of all three singing together. Pleased instead of panic-stricken at what he had wrought, Nick moved on to Verdi. From an old set of *Trovatore* the gold-rush chest-voice of Zinka Milanov reached to thrill me. Wagner was introduced through Lotte Lehmann and Lauritz Melchior singing the love duet from *Tristan*. Next came Wotan's farewell and the magic fire music from *Die Walküre*, conducted by Knappertsbusch, whose always-advancing quietness I was taught to value above the vertical clamour of Solti's complete *Ring*, released on Decca that very year. My prejudice against Solti – justified, I still believe, in the case of Wagner – was to remain fervent for years afterwards, until the lyrical flow of his *Eugene Onegin* made me think again. But prejudices were part of the enthusiasm, just as jealousy is part of passion. I went opera mad, and all because of Nick. He knew where to drop the needle – an especially important qualification in the matter of Wagner, with whom it is an invariable rule that the most immediately accessible bits are never at the edge of the disc.

Then there was Mozart. 'Lisa della Casa,' Nick would say, lying back in a winged chintz-covered chair with his eyes closed and his fingertips together, 'is a bear of very little brain, but you have to remember that *so was Wolfgang's wife.*' And at that moment, on the highlights record drawn from the wonderful old Erich Kleiber set of *Le nozze di Figaro*, the lady in question would sing the first notes of '*Dove sono*' for the tenth time on the trot. I wallowed like a hippo. It was a mud-bath in concentrated beauty. One doesn't love literature, said Flaubert. Though he said so because he was re-inventing it and the labour hurt, he would have been right anyway. Music we can love.

But the gramophone was merely an adjunct. The main means of instruction was the opera house itself. We were in the amphitheatre or the gods at Covent Garden almost every night. The nights we weren't, we were at Sadler's Wells, getting into training with the English version for something that would show up in the real language at the Garden later on. Nick was in no doubt about the Englishing of a foreign opera: it was strictly a leg-up for getting to grips with the original, in which the language was not just inseparable from the melody but formed its living spine. During the intervals of *Falstaff* we would adjourn to the bar so that Nick could discuss with his friends how Tito Gobbi or Geraint Evans was handling

the big challenge. Nick's friends called each other 'love'
a lot but they were all omniscient, so I assumed that they
had good reasons for booing Galina Vishnevskaya at
several points during *Aida*. Later on, however, I started
to wonder whether it hadn't been because she was show-
ing too much leg.

Because Nick's friends were queer without exception.
Or, rather, with one exception: me. Whether through
innocence or an opportunistic disinclination to compli-
cate such a rich source of free enlightenment, I failed for
a long time to rumble Nick's true sexual allegiance. The
young sailors who arrived at midnight and disappeared
into his bedroom would reappear at breakfast. Perhaps he
was picking up extra money teaching a workers' extension
course. Noises of wrestling came through the wall at
night. Perhaps he was practising judo. At long last I
realised why Nick wore such a forced smile when Robin
came to call. Indeed it was Robin who told me. She also
told me how unfair I was being. It wasn't just because I
had nothing with which to pay the rent that I was getting
away with paying no rent. Nor did all those tickets for
Covent Garden grow on trees. Even when you sat so high
in the gods that the stage looked like a postage stamp
crawling with ants, it still cost a lot of money to be present
on the night Birgit Nilsson kept drilling Brünnhilde's
climactic notes right through the middle while Valhalla,
which was supposed to fall, got caught in the scrim up
which the Rhine, in the form of projected green light, was
supposed to rise. She sang like a train coming while the
set malfunctioned all around her. It was heroic art and
it all had to be paid for. Nick was allowing himself to be
taken advantage of, but I was still taking advantage.
Once again it was time to move on.

Yet I was moving on with two acquisitions that would
serve me well. One was an awakened love for the exultant
human voice. The other was a reinforced tolerance for
homosexuality. Previously I had never been against it,

but had shared the usual delusion that it must be some sort of disease. After living with Nick and receiving the benefit of his knowledgeable, critical, yet wholeheartedly dedicated love of music, I came to believe that it was a necessary and valuable part of life. Two of my great heroes, Proust and Diaghilev, would have convinced me eventually. Proust's article about Flaubert, or that marvellous essay by Diaghilev in which he takes Benois to task for the deficiency of his historical view, would have been enough to persuade me that there is a quality of intellect, a generous precision of humane judgment, which, so far from being damaged by inverted sexual proclivities, is probably enhanced by them. But the job had already been done by a not always happy, always smiling school-teacher who so munificently showed me where to find, at the start of the second side of the Beecham set of *La Bohème*, the duet in which Victoria de los Angeles and Jussi Björling celebrate the beatific prospect of going to bed together. I still find it difficult to believe that Nick and his sailors felt the same way, but to believe otherwise would be an impertinence. Some people are different from the rest of us, and so are the rest of us.

14

Back to Square One

Homosexuality was not Dave Dalziel's problem. Many
people called him mad, but nobody ever called him queer.
You would have been able to tell he had arrived in
England just by how the girls at Melbury Road went
starry-eyed. They stopped giving each other haircuts
copied from Mary Quant advertisements and started
making group appointments at the hairdresser. Dalziel,
for as long as I cared to remember, had drawn women
like mosquitoes to a sleeping man. It wasn't because he
was good-looking, although he was. It wasn't because he
cleaned his nails and dressed in spruce clothes, although
he did. It was because he was obsessed. Dave Dalziel was
movie mad. He was determined to be a film director,
although there had been no Australian film director since
Charles Chauvel, mainly because there was no Australian
film industry. Very well, an Australian film industry
would have to be created.

Meanwhile Dalziel was in Europe to learn more about
the craft of his art. He had a short-subject script to shoot
and a rich friend, Reg Booth, who would finance the
project at the price of being allowed to star. Actually Reg
was rich only in comparison to the rest of us, so the
money had to be deployed with great care. Dalziel worked
all day on preparing this movie. In what spare time he
had he saw other movies. He breathed, ate and slept

movies. As a consequence, women went silly about him. It was because he had no time to be silly about them. The rest of us chased women and looked foolish doing it. He let them chase him and looked fine. I would have hated him for it if he had been less good company, but if you allowed for his occasional patch of near insanity he was too funny to pass up. Like all truly entertaining talkers he rarely told jokes. He just had a way of putting things. There was a big party on the top floor at Melbury Road to mark the official end of summer. Dalziel suddenly materialised and addressed me as if we had parted only the day before.

'I hear you've been living with a horse's hoof,' he drawled. It emerged that he and Reg had just taken a flat in Warwick Road, on the other side of Kensington High Street, and were looking for a third man to share the rent. 'Here's your chance to play Harry Lime. Also we need someone to keep the landlady quiet, who is a MONSTER. How would you like to slip her the pork sword?'

He always talked like that. The metaphors were so mind-boggling that you found yourself doing what he wanted. A dominant personality doesn't have to believe in its own will. All it needs is the inability to recognise the existence of anybody else's. My suitcase and several string-handled paper shopping bags full of books were downstairs in the hall. Dave, Reg and Robin helped me carry them to Warwick Road, although Robin, to my annoyance, clearly would have been glad to carry the whole lot just to be near Dave. Reg won't mind my saying this, because many times in the following year we bent elbows at the pub for the specific purpose of discussing Dalziel's demoralisingly unfair share of charm, which we were agreed gave rise to, or was possibly even caused by, grave simplicities in the brain. Reg also won't mind my saying that his script was no world-shaker. Even as I moved into the Warwick Road flat, principal photography was about to begin. From the way Mrs McHale, the middle-aged and bitterly irascible landlady, stood permanently by the staircase with her arms folded, you could tell that a top-floor flat with three heterosexual young Australian men in it was already well beyond the limits of what she would ordinarily be prepared to put up with. If her lips had been any more pursed they would have fallen off. You could also tell, from the way she tapped her prominently veined and sinewed foot, that she thought the young men had too many visitors even in normal circumstances – especially female visitors, whose presence necessitated her taking up an invigilating position on the landing outside our flat so that she could make frequent unannounced entrances through the door compulsorily left open. In the week before the camera turned on page one of the script there were a lot more visitors of both sexes. Mrs McHale's foot became a blur. Young actresses auditioning as extras arrived in miniskirts which Mrs McHale clearly regarded, not without reason, as tantamount to nudity. Men with silver boxes full of hired equipment and tea-chests full of scavenged props endangered the threadbare carpets and crappy wallpaper which Mrs McHale cherished as if the Victoria and Albert Museum could be restrained from appropriating them to its collection only by armed force. We called her Hearty McHale, in the way that a wrathful deity is given nicknames to make it less awful. What she was calling us was beyond guessing, but at the annual World Landladies' Rally in the Munich beer hall she would no doubt have plenty to say when her turn came at the banked microphones. 'They get like that,' said Dave wisely, 'when they don't get enough of the veal dagger.'

Applying listlessly for jobs during that period, I had plenty of spare time to help with the movie, and for acting as substitute focus-puller while playing a small part I got ten pounds for each week of the fortnight it took to shoot. The film, written by Reg with additional dialogue by

Dave, was a mystery about an unnamed man, played by Reg, who works as a hit-man for the Organisation and then finds out that the Organisation is trying to eliminate him, etc. Called *The Man from the Organisation*, it would have been the least mysterious mystery in the world if not for my focus-pulling, which gave some of the shots – the really vital ones, too expensive to be done again – an extra quality of ambiguity. Yet my acting was precise, even pedantic. In the key scene where I impersonated a passer-by in the street who turns to look at the seriously wounded hero, I walked the prescribed eighteen paces, paused for the three seconds required, and turned looking puzzled, exactly as instructed. Next day's rushes showed how exact I had been. You could see me silently counting to eighteen, moving my lips as I counted to three, and then looking as if I had been asked to expound Heisenberg's uncertainty principle. 'You'll have to do it again tomorrow unless we can get George C. Scott,' said Dave, making a note. 'Asking you to play someone you're not is like asking King Kong to play the Moonlight Sonata.' He was right. In later years my acting has improved, if only in the sense that I have got better at being myself.

During that hectic fortnight I learned a little about filming and a lot about Dalziel. I could see now that he wasn't always mad. Sometimes he was just concentrating. When he ignored what you were talking about and started a new conversation in the middle of your sentence, it was because he hadn't heard you. He attacked one crisis after another without any sign of artistic temperament. In sharp distinction to the rest of us, he didn't behave like an artist at all. He behaved like a truck-driver who has to get a load of perishable goods to a certain destination by a certain time. His creative resources were considerable, but invisible because fully committed. There was nothing left over with which to pose. Perhaps the logistic demands of his medium had matured him early. In my own medium, which makes few practical demands beyond the securing of an adequate supply of stationery, coming down to earth takes longer. But here again, and as usual, it was probably a matter of personality. Dave was simply the way he was. Once his single-mindedness had looked like dementia. Now it looked like obduracy. It didn't take a prophet to realise that one day it would look like talent.

Photography completed, *The Man from the Organisation* moved into what Dave called its post-production phase. In other words work stopped completely while they figured out how to pay for the editing. Reg was no longer rich and had to get a job as a driver with a luxury hire-car firm. This came in handy for allaying the spleen of Hearty McHale, because when Reg temporarily parked a Daimler or a Bentley in front of the house she got the idea that at least one of us was in funds. Reg spoiled it all one evening by forgetting to take off his cap. Dave, with characteristic practicality, had already arranged a short-term job in a Hammersmith builder's yard called Cornwall's Erections. He had underestimated, however, the physical labour involved. At sunset he would come reeling home too tired to wash off the grime. Usually there was some adoring woman who had been hanging around with no other aim in life beyond swabbing the caked dirt off his shoulders and bowed neck. When there wasn't, Reg and I took over. Even with these emollient side-benefits the job was clearly another case of Dalziel's extraordinary dedication to the task in hand. It made me feel queasy about borrowing money from him. Most of what I had earned from filming was already owed, which induced an anxiety that made me smoke more. Nor could it be denied that Warwick Road was situated less in Kensington than in Earls Court. I was back to where I had started, except lower down. Winter was almost upon us and I felt like the pariah of the pack. Even Robin, most generous of attendant angels, was looking at me with a curled lip.

Luck landed me my best job yet. A long, insane letter I had written to Penguin Books suggesting that they publish my collected works – I had left it unclear whether these as yet existed – won me an interview with one of their junior editors, a sleepily bright PhD type in her late twenties. Called Leslie, she immediately sussed that I was a bull artist but kindly suggested I might lower my sights and apply for a newly created menial job which would involve looking after the file of authors' photographs. Two heavily academic Pelicans had recently been published, written by Professor J. M. Thompson and Professor L. N. Thompson respectively. L. N. Thompson's photograph had ended up on J. M. Thompson's book and vice versa. One of them had been nice about it but insistent. The other had been merely insistent. The cost of stripping the covers off both editions and starting again had been very large, hence the decision to put the matter beyond doubt. Coached by Leslie, who advised the Singapore suit and my disintegrating but respectable pair of Chelsea boots with the chisel toes, I put in for the job and actually got it. I didn't tell them that I would be going up to Cambridge the year after next or even next year if I could swing it. Perhaps I was calculating that Penguin would go into liquidation in the near future or that my well-attested capacity to screw up would militate against permanence, but more likely I was just being, without particularly meaning to, deceitful. It can get to be a reflex.

The job was a cushy number. Once I had the few hundred photographs sorted into the right envelopes and the envelopes arranged in alphabetical order, all I had to do was sit there in my cubicle, wait until a request came down for a picture of, say, Malraux, and then make sure I didn't send them a picture of Maurois, Maurras, Mauriac, A. L. Rowse or Mel Tormé. You had to be careful with the Bloomsbury bunch because they all looked the same, as in a horse-breeder's catalogue. Otherwise it was a doddle. The only drawback was that Penguin's combined office, factory and warehouse was located in Harmondsworth, near Heathrow. The journey each way had to be done by Volkswagen Kombibus, from and to, in my case, a pick-up point in Cromwell Road. Among the dozen people on the bus there was always the languorously aloof Leslie. The driver of the bus was called Ted and was in most respects indistinguishable from Fred, the feeble-minded fascist of the Holloway Road light-metal factory, except that Ted had a richer source of material, namely the multi-ethnic pedestrian population of the London pavements. Looking everywhere except straight ahead, he never drew breath. 'Oo, lookit a nig-nog. Nar, ease a greasy wop. Garn, you poxing wog, get out of it . . .' The minibus load of liberal young ex-Oxbridge editors cast their eyes resignedly to heaven. Leslie regularly did her best to shut him up but always with adverse results, stupidity being the source of his motive power. If he couldn't curse, he couldn't drive. He had to spout his racist filth or the van would drift to a halt. I liked the way it bothered her. Me it amused. He was perfect, and anyway I believed, erroneously, that it was only the quiet men who were the real killers.

The working week took on a nice rhythm. After breakfast with the boys I would catch the bus, listen to Ted, look at Leslie, barricade myself into my cubicle and doze off, stirring only to work on a poem or take a long, slow look at a photograph of T. S. Eliot in order to eliminate the possibility that it was George Eliot in trousers. Lunch in the canteen offered virtually unobstructed views of Leslie. In the warehouse it was more or less obligatory to steal books: there was a pulp box in which you could find defective copies of almost any title, and usually the defects amounted to no more than a few pages inaccurately trimmed. Back to the cubicle for a read and a sleep. Then home in the bus, with the prospect of watching

Leslie getting stroppy with Ted. I liked her principles. I liked her wrists.

If the working day had a somnolent rhythm, the nights and the weekends were hyperactive. Even Dave, once he had been helped out of his inky bath, was always ready for the party. The party was never at our place, because Hearty McHale, rather than see us enjoy ourselves, would have called for an air strike to destroy her own house. But there was always a party on at least one floor of the house in Melbury Road. You could hear the music from the end of the street.

Journalists were writing a lot of stuff about the Sixties by that time. Harold Wilson was not only Prime Minister, he was still popular. He was not only still popular, he was almost credible: preaching the white heat of technology, he was Prometheus in Hush Puppies. A nation whose technology was white from frost-bite warmed itself at his words. The glossy magazines carried more articles each month about the new aristocracy of the classless cockney photographers in whose hairy arms the creamiest women of café society lay helpless. The articles were illustrated with photographs of the photographers taken by the photographers themselves. The pictures were very contrasty, making the women's faces look like Kabuki masks, while the photographers looked like East End criminals. There were pictures of East End criminals looking like company directors. In the text there was invariably a lot of talk about the disappearance of class divisions, the adduced evidence being that a pacey young designer from Tower Hamlets had married a duke's daughter. There would be a picture of the duke's daughter wearing the young designer's designs. Located without any connecting tissue inside the perimeter of the bleached-out facial area, her enormous black-rimmed eyes and grainy grey mushroom mouth looked surprised at her own daring: three blots on white cardboard. The vacant were being given *carte blanche* to adore themselves.

Once the enviable had looked human but hard to get at. Now they looked inhuman and further off than ever.

For those of us with our noses pressed to the glass, the reality of the swinging new era was a dance party to which you brought your own bottle. But as the news about the allegedly effervescent London reached Australia, ship-loads of would-be revellers and social revolutionaries came sailing towards the putative action. Inevitably they all ended up at the bottle party. People I had left Australia to get away from started turning up in bunches – intellectuals who had read three books; writers who had read no books at all and would never write one either; pub singers who would forget the words of their sea-shanties unless you were unlucky. They filed on to the buses at Southampton and debouched into Earls Court by the well-drilled platoon.

Less organised on principle but no more reticent, those members of the Downtown Push who were still young enough to travel arrived in dribs and drabs. The woodwork was the whole world thick but out of it they came crawling, still full of theories about the repressive mechanisms of a society which allowed them to indulge their every whim. Grecian Ern Papadakis arrived, his famous book on Trotsky as yet unpublished, mainly because it remained unwritten. Not far behind him came Ross Peters the Prestige Pie-eater, an expert on Reich's orgone theories who had once received a letter from Reich himself. There men were legends and had the women to prove it: lank-haired, taciturn creatures with approximately depilated bare legs, their shoulders hunched from constant listening.

One night at Melbury Road, half cut and wholly content in the midst of the writhing throng, I had just finished shaking to a Beatles track when I was horrified to hear the actual living squeal of Johnny Pitts, the Push folk-singer who had for ten years unsuccessfully attempted to emigrate from Australia so as to go to South America and – I quote the wording of his passport application – fight for anarchy. At last they had made the mistake of letting him out, and now he was here. As usual he thrashed his guitar, whined a few bars about bad working conditions in some American correctional facility, and fell sideways. Somebody put the Beatles back on and the crowded room danced again, but it had been a bad moment. Sitting exhausted in a corner with a woman kneeling at each arm and another soothing his forehead from behind, Dalziel suddenly looked haunted. The past was catching up.

But you could always outrun it. One place we ran to was the Iron Bridge Tavern, deep in the East End. Queenie Watts and a friend of hers called Shirley sang jazz there every Saturday. We used to go down there in Dingo Kinsella's apology for a car. Dingo was a spidery journalist serving a one-year stretch in the London bureau of one of the Sydney newspapers. This meant that he was being paid an Australian salary, which in turn meant that he was, by our standards, wealthy. If he had drunk less seriously he would have been driving a Facel Vega at the very least. As things were, he locomoted in what must have been the last roadworthy example of the old upright Ford Popular. A car that had never been popular with anybody I knew of, it held all of us in acute discomfort. Dingo drove the way he drank, as if he wanted to die. But since the Popular's top speed wasn't much higher than that of a walking man, we were all agreed that it was worth the risk. Every Saturday, Dingo would give three toots on the horn and we would all pile out of the house to go looking for the car in the next street. Hearty McHale refused to let him park the machine even momentarily in front of her salubrious establishment, lest property values should be lowered still further.

On the way down the long East India Dock Road to the pub the car would weave from side to side in a sine curve of about ten feet amplitude and a hundred feet pitch. At the Iron Bridge we would listen to the happily shouting trad band until time was called and we were thrown out. On the road home the car ran straight and level, because when Dingo got blotto beyond a certain point he seized up solid. Turning corners remained a problem, which we could sometimes solve by getting him to close his eyes and talking him through it. In a faster car this would have been fatal. To us it was just part of what Bruce Jennings might have called a Rewarding Experience for the Young People.

15

The Green Gladiolus

Dressed as a deliberate caricature of an English gentle-man from the late gasolier period, Bruce Jennings had been in London longer than anyone and was both ap-palled and delighted that the rest of Australia now seemed bent on joining him. He was appalled because, without being in any way servile, he had submitted himself to Europe and was by now ten years deep into a love affair that the new arrivals looked determined to consummate in five minutes. He was delighted because they provided him with raw material. I suppose Reg and myself were included in his field of observation. But Jennings' interest in Dave was more than just clinical. He recognised a fellow talent. His memories of home sharpened by exile, Jennings was the first Australian writer-performer to exploit the Australian idiom for its full poetic value. He had a fine ear and the learning to back it up. Dave, though an avid general reader, had only the ear. But Jennings valued Dave's ability to fish a phrase up out of childhood and throw it flapping on the table. 'Fair suck of the pineapple,' Dave would say in protest when I tried to hit him for a quid at Wally's, and Jennings' eyes would go shiny. He'd forgotten that one.

Wally's was the greasy spoon in a lane behind Warwick Road. It served plates of fat. You could have sausages in your fat or fried eggs in your fat. You could have the sausages and the fried eggs together, but it meant you got more fat. We ate at Wally's most evenings because the price of cooking at home was a stream of protest notes from Hearty McHale about noise, smells, smoke, fire and the lettuce leaf so vandalously trodden into the hallway carpet. Wally's was a strange place to find the fastidious Jennings – who was known to take luncheon at Rules in the company of his admirer, John Betjeman – but he dropped in a couple of times during the period when he and Dave were discussing the possibility of a movie. I secretly laughed this possibility to scorn, not yet having realised that the ability to plan in the long term, while retaining the capacity to tell a long-term plan from a wild dream, is crucial to success in any of the collaborative arts. I thought they were both a bit nuts.

Jennings left you in no doubt of his brilliance, though in some fear that his monologues might never end. A career drinker, he would stand balefully in the middle of a party, the only man present in a Turnbull & Asser shirt, antique Chavet tie, pin-stripe double-breasted Savile Row suit, Lobb shoes, black fedora and a monocle. 'Des is the name,' he would loudly confide to an invisible interlocutor, 'Des Esseintes.' And indeed he was the hero of *A Rebours* to the life, a Count Robert de Montesquiou *de nos jours*, creating himself as a work of art. He didn't have the living tortoise inset with turquoises but no doubt it was on order. Meanwhile he had everything else, and I was wide-eyed even as he stood there swaying. When he fell to the floor he would usually take a couple of people with him. Laid to rest on a sofa, he would sleep until the party thinned out. Then, with just the right-sized audience, he would start a closed-eyed, resonant muttering which might consist of nothing but brand-names and radio jingles from the far Australian past. 'Rosella Tomato Sauce . . . Twice As Nice If Kept On Ice . . . Sydney Flour is our flour, we use it every day . . . I like Aeroplane Jelly, Aeroplane Jelly for me . . . You'll sleep tight 'cause you'll sleep right, on a Lotusland inner-spring mattress . . .'

Years later I was to realise that this was the most original side of his mind talking. He was rediscovering and reordering an Australian language which had never had any pretensions beyond the useful and had thus retained an inviolable purity. It was the language written on bottles of cough medicine and packets of junket powder: a vocabulary without any value beyond common currency, and therefore undiluted by aesthetic pretension. With a sure instinct reinforced by his dandyish collector's erudition, he had realised that not all the ephemeral was evanescent – that there was such a thing as a poetry of trivia, uniquely evocative for a country whose art was hag-ridden by a self-conscious striving towards autonomous respectability. Jennings was already well embarked on a salvage expedition to raise a nation's entire cultural subconscious. The obtuse among his country's intellectuals – a high proportion – thought he was lowering the tone, and belittled him accordingly. He armoured himself by polishing his façade still more brightly. Delacroix, said the doomed Jean Prévost in his wonderful book about Baudelaire, was a dandy not because he wanted to impose his superiority but because he wanted to defend it. Similarly Jennings retreated ever further into his own effulgence, taunting his detractors with the dazzling pages of an open book – the lexicon of their lost youth.

At the time, however, I couldn't get interested in any of that, since it concerned Australia, and Jennings' Australia, through being so vivid, only lit up what I was still trying to leave. It was Jennings' Europe that attracted me. Jennings could tell you what Satie had said about Ravel. I knew what Hemingway had said about Gertrude Stein, but Jennings knew what Gertrude Stein had said about Picabia, because he owned the letters. He also owned a Picabia. For Jennings, the side-trails of the old international avant-garde were a stamping ground. I thought then, and still think now, that it is more important to be familiar with the major artistic works than knowingly conversant with the minor artists, but Jennings wasn't as easy to fault there as one might have thought. Just because he knew a lot about Honegger didn't mean that he was an ignoramus about Haydn. Jennings was formidable. I didn't envy him his talent, being conceited enough to believe that I had some of my own. I did envy him his well-stocked mind. Actually I should have envied him his talent too: stocking your mind isn't the same as stacking crates in a warehouse. It's a gift.

So is being a landlady. Either you run the show, or the show runs you. Hearty McHale was determined to be mistress in her own house. It followed ineluctably that we were on borrowed time. We were careful to have no parties. We rarely cooked anything more complicated than half a pound of frankfurts. But we were an epicentre of unpredictability. Hearty McHale's mental equilibrium depended on a silent house full of closed doors, with nothing moving except rent. The only acceptable noise in her establishment was the restrained clamour made by money as it transferred itself from the tenant's wallet into the owner's bank account. From there, according to rumour, the loot went to Spain and was sunk into a block of flats affording a view of the sea to any British mountain-climbing holiday-maker equipped with powerful binoculars.

Such was the system which our mere presence disturbed. If we had been trainee Trappists we might have lasted longer. As things were, the crisis came closer every day. In the evenings I would stagger upstairs with heaps of Penguin books for my growing library. When one of these heaps collapsed in my arms, an extruded copy of *The Psychopathology of Everyday Life* inflicted minor but detectable damage on the hallway rubber plant. Hearty

McHale reacted as if I had thrown a phosphorous gren-
ade. She had already warned me that the beams under
my area of the floor were not designed to hold up the
British Museum reading room. Books, however, were a
negligible irritant compared with women. Reg had a very
quiet Australian girl-friend whom he planned to, and
subsequently did, marry. Mostly he visited her instead
of she him, but she turned up in Warwick Road on
two occasions and for Hearty McHale two meant two
hundred. Robin came to me at least once a week because
it was not practicable for me to take to her the clothes
that needed ironing, darning, mending, replacing, etc.
Unless these missions of mercy could be accurately timed
by the synchronisation of watches and the use of sema-
phor from the top window, they necessarily entailed the
ringing of the downstairs front doorbell, which Hearty
McHale interpreted as the prelude to nuclear attack.

But it was Dave's female admirers who tipped the
already precarious balance. When he loved them and left
them, some of them failed to get the point, and came
looking for him. Reg and I spent a lot of time sitting in
the kitchen with a lissome yet decidedly hysterical actress
called Bambi who was reluctant to believe that Dave had
had to depart suddenly for Easter Island. Leaving one
cigarette still smouldering in the ashtray on the kitchen
table, she would light several others while compulsively
searching the flat. Reg would trail her, catching the
ash in his cupped hands before it hit Hearty McHale's
moth-eaten though purportedly invaluable carpet. Dave
was curled up in the loft above the bathroom. He was so
tired after a day's work at Cornwall's Erections that he
didn't care where he slept, so it was all right for him. But
it was tough on us, and finally we rebelled. Perhaps we
were offended by what he could afford to turn down. An
evening came when we declined to stall Bambi and she
caught him still in the bath. It was the luxury bubble-bath
we gave him each Friday. Friday was pay-day and we

would count his money as he lay in deep foam after another dedicated week of selfless toil. Taking the sponge from me and the loofah from Reg, Bambi arrogated to herself the task of cleansing and anointing the exhausted hero. Reg and I retreated to the kitchen for half a bottle each of Woodpecker cider, a few hands of gin rummy and some ill-disguised fits of jealousy. When Hearty McHale burst in, her pulsatingly veined feet were about six inches off the linoleum, thus indicating the speed she had attained going up the final flight of stairs. She evinced the special fury reserved for when it was Dave who was receiving the female visitor. Brushing our feeble reassurances aside, she headed for the bathroom, with Reg and me close behind her and making as much noise as possible so that Dave might take warning. The bathroom door was locked from inside but Hearty McHale had a ring of duplicate keys, like a warder. She threw open the door. Bambi was nowhere to be seen. Dave sat there in deep white suds looking suitably shocked. Some of the items in his pile of discarded clothes were suspiciously diaphanous at a second glance but otherwise there was no sign of anything untoward. Had he lowered her out of the window on a rope of knotted towels?

The long, interrogative silence was broken by the splutter of Bambi surfacing. Mesmerised by her cap, epaulettes and half-cup brassière of glistening foam, I had a pang of envy that I can still feel as I write this. Reg positioned himself to catch Hearty McHale's falling body but she was made of sterner stuff than that. The network of veins stood out in relief from the tops of her feet like the roots of gum-trees on the bank of a dry creek, but if standing on your dignity is what really matters, you can even have apoplexy in the upright position. Skinflint means what it says.

16

Autumn of the Expatriates

So we got notice one day and a new home the next. It was the house in Melbury Road, whose palatial ground-floor flat had suddenly become vacant after the landlady's husband died of old age. The landlady, who had run an all-female orchestra during an earlier incarnation, instantly moved into the basement, where she kept open sherry for any of the orchestra's alumnae still capable of dropping by. Her name was Geraldine and she was, for a landlady, unusually accommodating, probably because of her close spiritual connection with 'hot' music, a renowned sweetener of the soul. An already heavily peopled house was thus made free to rival the demographic density of Shanghai. There were three floors of Australian girls above us, Geraldine and her heavily lisping visiting female ex-clarinettists below us, and Dibbs Buckley living in the backyard studio with his gorgeous wife Delish – a name whose accent fell on the second syllable because it was short for delicious.

The backyard studio had been added when the house was owned by one of the Pre-Raphaelites – either Holman Burne-Jones or Edward Everett Hunt, I can never remember which, having conceived, as you might have gathered, a hatred for the Brotherhood and all their works which has endured to this day. But the Pre-Raphs knew how to look after themselves. The studio was a split-level pavilion befitting Buckley's status as incomparably the most successful young Australian expatriate. Sidney Nolan had taken decades to break through but Dibbs, while the dust from the rubble was still rising, made his entrance through the same hole with a Qantas bag over his shoulder. The Marlborough Gallery was selling his pictures as fast as he could paint them, which was very fast indeed, because he worked in sequences. Golden-haired, rugby-nosed and as restless as a surfer on a wet day, he chose a theme, painted every possible variation on it, and then sold his sketchbooks and preliminary drawings along with the pictures. Before sending the drawings off for sale he would deck them out with quotations from his current reading. Privately I thought this practice a slightly premature assumption of immortality but publicly I smoked his expensive cigars and drank his even more expensive imported Australian beer, while doting, like every other red-blooded male of Dibbs's acquaintance, on the seraphically lovely Delish – an admiration which in my case she didn't pretend to reciprocate. Mortification was eased by the fact that she plainly didn't care much for any of us. Unusually for a woman, she didn't favour even Dave with a soft eye. She would smile at him occasionally, but it was only a refrigerator door opening.

Delish was a van Eyck angel in jeans and T-shirt, but she had a hard business brain and could spot anyone who would waste her husband's time a mile off. Dibbs's propensity to sit around drinking and yarning with his less luminous fellow countrymen she regarded as a tolerable, or at any rate inevitable, subsidiary urge, but she had a clock running somewhere in the background and always made sure he was dead on time for dinner with Sir Kenneth Clark. At the end of the day's work, if the late autumn weather was fine, we would gather around the great oak in front of the studio to drink away our respective memories of Penguin Books, luxury cars that broke down on the M1, the rigours of Cornwall's Erections and an enormously demanding sequence of paintings about Christine Keeler and Mandy Rice-Davies. The arguments were more heated than illuminating. Dibbs would hail the greatness of Matisse, I would explain that Matisse was essentially derivative, Dibbs would correctly insist that the *circa* 1906 Matisses in Leningrad were of an unparalleled grandeur, and I would pour scorn all the more eloquently for not having been to Leningrad and knowing nothing about the subject. Meanwhile Dave had the blacked-out look he got when he was mentally working on a screen-play and Reg wondered openly how these egomaniacs could breathe the same air. It was a pleasant pastime, which for the rest of us went on after Delish had appeared, whispered in Dibbs's ear, and taken him inside. But when, half an hour later, the two of them would emerge transformed – Dibbs in a dinner jacket with his aureate locks carefully tousled, Delish in silver sandals and some dream of a plum-juice silk sheath held up by nothing but her perfect breasts – the pastime was shattered by reality. They were off to the opera and we weren't. The dregs in the tins of beer tasted like aloes.

But the air of prosperity emanating from the backyard studio was contagious. Before winter had taken its grip, Dalziel had signed off from Cornwall's Erections and signed on as a supply teacher. Reg handed in his chauffeur's cap and took the same route to respectability. Though they never knew what school they would be teaching at tomorrow there was usually work, and, more important, always a decent pay-packet. Australian supply teachers were in good repute, especially if they taught English, because among the natives the ability to spell and parse their own language was already becoming scarce. Each morning the three of us left for work looking the height of bourgeois conformity. My beard was still in place but the effect was tempered by Reg's spare tweed jacket, which he eventually let me have at a low price after I had burned a hole in the sleeve. At the end of the day we would converge again out of the cold, exhaling puffs of steam but with enough spare energy to get on with real life. I worked at my poems, Reg chipped away at the opening sentence of a novel which might well be finished by now, and Dave, with Dingo's willing co-operation, transported the increasingly less rough assembly of *The Man from the Organisation* from one borrowed editing room to another. Dinner was meat – not hunks of meat, as in Australia, but pathetic scraps of meat, as in Britain – which the girls upstairs transformed into edible dishes by heating it in secret ways and adding bits of stuff to it. There was a lot of wine. The evening usually grew into a party. Life had acquired a certain rhythm.

Spencer disrupted it. When left behind in Australia, he had been bisexual, broke, and an expert at wasting his outstanding verbal gift. Now, suddenly, he was married to an heiress, had arrived in London by aircraft, possessed money to burn, and was set on making the West End the jumping-off point for an assault on world theatre. He wanted me to collaborate with him on the writing of a revue. Once written, the show would be financed by his wife's father, whose name in Australia was synonymous with a brand of fly-paper which hung in every home. For almost fifty years (Pam, Spencer's wife, was a child of the tycoon's third, or it could have been fourth, marriage) money had been accumulating in the family vault with the tempo and volume of flies hitting sticky paper across Australia's three million square miles of hot rock. Now the cash would be put to creative use. Spencer explained all this to me while he manoeuvred a second-hand but sumptuous Armstrong-Siddeley Sapphire towards the terrace house he and Pam had taken in Hampstead. A whole floor of the house had been fitted out as a study. High-quality cigarettes and alcohol, purchased on Spencer's Harrods account, stood within reach of a casual hand. The typewriter was the size of a grand piano. Here we settled down one Saturday and discussed what we were going to write. We were still discussing it on Sunday. Pam did the cooking, which consisted principally of examining the tin of jellied pheasant until she found the instructions for getting it open. Spencer and I did the talking. Nobody did any actual writing but it was early days and careful planning was held to be a virtue. The show, provisionally called *The Charge of the Light Fandango*, would galvanise the comic theatre out of the complacency into which it had been plunged by the inexplicable success of *Beyond the Fringe*. Spencer and I found it hard to agree about most things but on that point we concurred: the audience must not be truckled to. The current fad for undergraduate irreverence, we knew, merely flattered their philistine self-satisfaction. We would provide something less palatable.

But success lay in the future – rather further in the future than either of us could possibly imagine. Meanwhile here was a quasi-creative way of justifying a succession of drunken winter weekends. One could get smashed and call it a theatrical experiment. Theatre, always absurdly overvalued in London, was at that time spoken of with religious awe. Some of the older actors deserved the worship they attracted. I saw Gielgud in *The Cherry Orchard* and thought him as good as the play. Somehow I got to Chichester and saw Olivier's Othello. When he ripped the crucifix from his neck and flung it aside, you knew that it had flown straight down the gangway to his dressing-room and hung itself on a hook: the physical energy was volcanic but precise, like his articulation of the words, which his super-spade accent coated with bitter chocolate but did not blur. *Put out delight and den put out delight*. Exactly what he did put out, the sexy devil.

Alas, it was already the twilight of the great actors. The producer was the new king. This was all right if the gimmick fitted: Peter Hall's *Troilus and Cressida*, previously known as Shakespeare's *Troilus and Cressida*, lost nothing by being put on in a sand-tray and Dorothy Tutin looked good barefooted, kicking granular silicon all over the Americans in the front stalls. For Peter Brook's all-leather *King Lear*, however, Paul Scofield had been encouraged to adopt a gravel voice. From the circle of the Aldwych I couldn't hear what he was talking about. He looked like Tugboat Annie on a wet night and sounded like a cement mixer. Even worse, the director had run the first three acts together without an interval. There was no way of knowing this fact in advance unless you had bought a programme and I had bought a couple of extra pints of bitter instead. In the exact centre of a very long row of people, by the end of the first act I was ready for a pee. By the end of the second act I was ready for emergency surgery. When the third act followed without a break I knew that something would have to be done, possibly *in situ*. I held out as long as I could and then started crawling across people's knees. On stage, Gloucester was having his eyes put out. In the circle, there was a man struggling desperately sideways towards the exit through an entanglement of legs, like one of those American footballers in training who have to run very fast with knees high through piles of tyres.

I made it to safety approximately in time, but as I stood there – or, rather, reeled and swayed there like a man watering his lawn with a hose which had been unexpectedly connected to a powerful artesian well – it began to strike me that the capacity of my bladder was perhaps incompatible with the quantities of liquid I was attempting to put into it. Over the next decade I attempted to solve this problem by forcing even more liquid in, on the assumption that this would enlarge the receptacle. Common sense, which might have suggested that this was the wrong approach, was vitiated by the method itself. When I finally embraced abstinence it was because of the simple urge to work a longer day. Thus, without joining Alcoholics Anonymous, I was at last able to leave Piss-Artists Notorious. But that's a much later story. At the time we are talking about, I was a man out of control, sobbing with relief in a urinal while the lights were going out on the Third Servant as he fetched flax and whites of eggs for Gloucester's bleeding face.

The return to my seat in the audience was effected by the same route employed on leaving it. At least nobody mistook my performance for part of the production. But following hard upon producer's theatre came the theatre of group improvisation, one of whose hallmarks was that the actors were practically never on the actual stage, but were continually roaming up and down the gangways looking for trouble. New York's Living Theater had come to town and its collectively inspired cast spent the whole time in the audience provoking hostile bourgeois response and thus unveiling the insidious nature of US imperialism, although there was rarely any mention of the especially insidious aspect of US imperialism represented by the Living Theater. London's typical literary couple – he a novelist, she a cookery correspondent or vice versa – would sit dutifully attentive in their aisle seats while a naked six-foot white actor with a beard, or a naked six-foot black actor without a beard but with an earring, thrust his bottom in their faces as a challenge to their honky values. Afterwards they would invite him home to insult them further, consume all the liquor in their stripped-pine drinks cabinet and violate their teenage daughter.

Dibbs and Delish Buckley varied from this practice only by inviting the whole cast. Our nostrils invaded by an unfamiliar sweet odour, Dave, Reg and I went out into the yard one chill night and found it inhabited by murmuring people in fancy dress, passing, after one dainty puff each, an oddly defeated-looking roll-your-own cigarette around in a circle. Having included herself for some reason in this silent pow-wow, Delish looked especially exotic, like a Dior mannequin in a hobo camp. Unasked yet vociferously confident, I joined the circle, making sure, when the butt got to me, that I dealt with it properly. I sucked it to a stub in two jumbo drags. 'Who is *this* asshole?' whispered a huge black man standing by the oak tree. I knew he was black because I couldn't see him against the dark trunk and I knew he was huge because the voice came from high up. Delish gave me one of those downward waves of the hand with which she customarily apologised for the provincial behaviour of her husband's hangers-on. She had beautiful hands, incidentally: deeply tanned but glowing with that edible, enviable golden health which Modigliani gave his odalisques while he was dying. Cruel one, I pursue thee over the rolling billows. Horace said that. Someone must have put him through it.

17

The Deep Tan Fades

The foundations of Delish Buckley's profound tan had been laid in Australia. That much went without saying. She and I had both been exposed to the same intensity and duration of ultra-violet. Even though she had done most of her elegantly splayed spine-bashing on the high-toned beaches north of Newport, whereas I had been mainly confined to the humbler inlets stretching south from Bondi to Cronulla, it had been the same free sunlight for both of us. But Delish's tan was now being topped up by regular visits to the Bahamas, St Tropez and – the Buckleys practically discovered the place – Bali. Her tan was intact. Mine was a memory. In Australia, even during winter, one had always had, when one examined oneself before the mirror, a tide-mark around one's waist and upper thighs. When naked, even at one's most wan, one had always looked, at the very least, as if one were wearing a nifty little pair of white panties. But after the second year in London the hallowed demarcation line paled away, never properly to return. Stripped to the waist on a summer's day in Holland Park, the most you could acquire was a mild pink blush. Jamaicans in Fair Isle beanies laughed as they danced past your out-stretched form. At night the pink rash itched like an authentic burn but declined to alter the skin's pigmentation. The melanin remained unmoved. You woke in the morning looking more than ever like a peeled raw potato about a week old, with a certain subtle tinge of azure to its chill whiteness. For the girls, the disaster could be staved off with a sun-lamp or, failing that, a timely application of Tan-Fastic. For the men, most of whom could barely afford to keep an ordinary electric bulb burning, there was nothing to do except become resigned. Turning pale was part of one's commitment to the great adventure.

As so often happens in matters of morale, to give up the symbol led to a wholesale erosion of the reality it stood for. When the Chindits in Burma lost hope, they gave up shaving, and when they gave up shaving they would die of a cut finger. When we lost our tan, the emblem of our bronzed Aussie robustness, we tended to yield along the whole front of general fitness and healthy diet. Dalziel was an exception: he had never smoked and always drank less than other people so that he could give them orders in a credible voice. The rest of us smoked as much as our credit would stand. My borrowing require-ment for cigarettes always ran at an unreal proportion of salary. Each time I shifted to smaller cigarettes, I upped the frequency with which I demolished them. By now I had left Players No. 6, the kiddies' cigarette, far behind, and was smoking some brand that looked as if it should have been dangling from the lower lip of a hamster. But I sucked them in like short lengths of spaghetti.

The steady kippering of my insides had so far led to only intermittent convulsions – the average coughing fit was easily quelled by squeezing my head between my knees – but my wind already showed signs of impair-ment. If I ran a hundred yards for a stationary bus I couldn't get up the stairs after I had caught it. Like most people who smoked umpteen cigarettes a day, I tasted only the first one. The succeeding umpteen minus one were a compulsive ritual which had no greater savour than the fumes of burning money. To have experienced the full thrill, one would have had to have been one's own girl-friend, for whom mouth-to-mouth contact clearly had the same effect as sucking the exhaust pipe of a diesel truck. Smoking so many more cigarettes than you felt like smoking was supposed to indicate an addiction to nicotine, but I suspect that in my case it was merely gluttony. Call it an addictive personality if you like, but since the age of nought I had never been able to get enough of anything. First it was milk and then it was marshmallows.

Just after the war my mother was invited to an RSL social evening in Kogarah. Whereas any man who had served in any capacity could be a full member of the Returned Servicemen's League, she, a war widow whose husband had died on active service, had to wait to be invited into the RSL hall as a guest. Such was the position of women in Australia at that time. One of the most prominent dignitaries of the local RSL lived in our street. He had spent the war as a quartermaster at Singleton, with special responsibility for latrine-boring equipment. My mother's inclination was to wish a plague on the whole business, but she wanted to give me a night out, and the social evening had a special supper for children. A highlight of the supper was marshmallows. Several of the children ate half a dozen of these each and felt sick. I swallowed two dozen and felt fine, except when my breathing stopped. Picked up from where I was writhing on the floor, I was held aloft by giant hands and slapped vigorously on the back. Nothing happened for some time, and then a pink-and-white mass of congealed marshmallows the size and splendour of a shampoo-soaked satin cushion from Zsa-Zsa Gabor's boudoir hit the floor with a sticky plop.

This pattern was to recur. I had better be silent about the ticklish matter of a certain famous pie, except to say that if that brand of meat pie had not been meant to be eaten in excess, its pastry would not have been so enticingly soggy, and that if the pie had not been meant to be regurgitated, the cubes of meat gleaming through its sludge of gravy would not have been so purple. But the RSL marshmallows and the meat pies happened in Australia, as an occasional alternative to good home cooking, and where the effects of *gourmandise* could be offset by exercise. In London there was no home cooking worthy of the name. When you were in funds you ate out. But only the people whose faces appeared in such publications as *Town* and *Queen* could afford to eat in restaurants serving food which would leave them looking and feeling better instead of worse. 'A way of life based on the glossy magazine,' Harold Macmillan had said in a bid to touch the common pulse, and his very words told you how remote the idea was from everyday experience.

When we felt rich, we ate in the local Angus Steak House, where a bland but plump piece of animal was accompanied by reasonably crisp chips and a half tomato cut with a toothed circumference, like a rubicund cogwheel. When we felt less rich, we might eat at a certain British chain of hamburger restaurants devoted to serving nothing else. In recent years, perhaps encouraged by competition from McDonald's, the British hamburger has become a credit to the nation. At the time of which I speak, it looked like a scorched beer-coaster or a tenderised disc brake. Flanked by chips which, if picked up individually on a fork, either shattered or else drooped until their ends touched, the British hamburger lay there sweltering under its limp grey duvet of over-fried onions. When you cut it up, put the pieces in your mouth and swallowed them, the British hamburger shaped itself to the bottom of your stomach like ballast, while interacting with your gastric juices to form an incipient belch of enormous potential, an airship which had been inflated in a garage. This belch, when silently released, would cause people standing twenty yards away to start examining the soles of their shoes. The vocalised version sounded like a bag of tools thrown into a bog.

The British hamburger thus symbolised, with savage neatness, the country's failure to provide its ordinary people with food which did anything more for them than sustain life. In Italy, for the same price as a typical British hamburger meal including sweet, a builder's labourer could eat like a king – rather better in fact, because pasta dishes gain from being kept simple. Françoise, short of lire herself, and with her slim resources cut in half by my presence, always took me where the poor ate well. In Britain this opportunity was not on the cards. It was said that a poor man could eat well in Britain if he ate a British Railways breakfast three times a day, but British Railways was already in the process of putting its breakfast beyond the reach of the average wage-earner – a process which was to culminate, after the name-change to British Rail, in a successful effort to put the same breakfast beyond the reach of the Duke of Westminster. A more practical alternative to the British hamburger – more practical than climbing on a train just to eat – was the workers' café, or kayf. Alas, not every district had one of these. At their best, the kayfs had a certain style. Men with flat caps, donkey jackets and chipped fingernails could fill up on beef and two veg plus spotted dick with custard. At their worst, the kayfs sliced the beef with the same sectioning equipment used to prepare laboratory specimens for mounting on a microscope slide. Even worse than the worst, there was Wally's, still bubbling away like a tub of hot fat in the lane behind Warwick Road, only a few hundred yards away from Melbury Road across Kensington High Street. All too often we would end up at Wally's because we were collectively too broke for any other solution except one: the last, the zero option, which was to eat at home.

This wasn't so bad when the girls on one of the floors above us did the cooking, but they weren't always available. Most evenings we would send an ambassador upstairs to explore the possibility of having our food cooked for us. Usually the girls would invite us all up and help transform our scrawny chops or dreadful packets of sausages and streaky bacon into something edible. But increasingly often they were lost in the throes of preparing a beef Stroganoff or a casserole, the centrepiece of some candle-lit dinner party for English suitors in charcoal pin-stripe suits. It got to the point where the girls would be wearing full-length gowns and jewellery. The Ruperts and Christophers would arrive in cabs full of roses. The stench of flowers on the stairs drove us back defeated into our all-male domain, where there was nothing to do except fend for ourselves, with predictable results. Supermarket food bred a supermarket mentality. I myself could account for a pound of pork sausages at a sitting. I don't know exactly what was in the sausages, but I did know that a block of ice-cream made by the same firm didn't taste significantly different.

Though Dalziel made sure he got to a health-food restaurant once a month, the rest of us ate junk because it was easy and I ate more junk than anybody because to keep on eating was easier than stopping. For brief spells the supervisory care of an accompanying woman led to a saner diet, but the only reason this happened was because letting her look after the food was easier than looking after it myself. It was the line of least resistance, and usually it led downwards. I had not yet begun to put on weight, but the possibility was there, like the side of a hill getting ready to slip. There was a falling feeling, especially in the scalp. My comb had hair in it. When the others told me I had a bald patch I told them it was an enlarged crown, but with a shaving mirror held at an angle over my head like a halo I looked into the bathroom mirror and saw a would-be tonsure about the size of a florin. American graduates in hair technology called this the 'O' effect. The 'O' effect at the back of my head was being approached by an 'M' effect at the front, where my temples, when I pulled the hair back from them with the edge of my hand, were retreating as I watched. Add this combination to my wrecked mouth, my all-over pallor and an escalating inability to make any sudden move without coughing for ten minutes, and you had a lot to worry about. And when you had a lot to worry about, the thing to do was to have a lot to drink.

Everybody I knew drank all the time, so I wasn't unusual in that. But I was unusual, I now see, in so easily getting drunk. I couldn't see it then because I was always either drunk or recovering. What I had was a ridiculously light head. I had no more business drinking alcohol than someone allergic to cheese has eating pizza. Unfortunately I liked the feeling of getting tight. When we all went down to the pub in the evenings, I discovered with intense pleasure that the revoltingly cheery horse-brass décor was already out of focus after the second pint of brown water. After the third pint I could barely articulate, and like most people in that condition I found articulation a matter of urgency. Trying to say something of extreme importance, I dimly registered that my tongue was moving slowly. So I started to say the same thing again, as if repetition would get the message across. At closing time it was a hundred-yard walk home for everybody else and about half a mile for me. Every few seconds I would spot the rest of the blokes and try to join them, but couldn't find them again until I had bounced off a brick wall or a parked car. The hangover next morning would be an epic. Overnight dehydration shrivelled my eyes to raisins. Every morning my tongue was like a small sand dune abraded by a hot wind.

Nowadays, more than ten years after swearing off the demon rum, I can take half an inch of wine with a meal without seizing the bottle from the waiter and tilting it to my pursed lips. Strictly speaking, therefore, I was never an alcoholic. I didn't need to be. Just as most people who take cocaine are not drug addicts, but behave so badly that they might as well be, so did I manifest every characteristic of the true booze artist. Except one: my leg wasn't hollow. Or to put it another way: my head wasn't hard enough to let my leg fill up. I got paralytic too quickly to do myself any major damage. The authentic toper bombs his brain-cells with a bottle of Scotch a day and you never notice until they take him away for a liver transplant. Me you noticed in the first few minutes. All the more unlikely, then, that the delicately poised Leslie should even contemplate an emotional alliance.

Yet it happened, although so briefly that I doubted its occurrence immediately afterwards. Probably I doubted its occurrence even during, and thus hastened its end. Though she was undemonstrative to the point of shyness, it was all too obvious that she was letting me into her life as a distraction from heartbreak. A long love affair with a married man was either reaching the usual conclusion or had entered one of the usual off-again hiatuses preceding the usual conclusion. The older and more experienced man having lost his charm, the way was open for the younger and less experienced man to pose his more easily thwarted threat. The door to her affections opened so suddenly that I can forgive myself for falling through it, but not for flailing straight across the room and toppling out of the window. Leslie would have had a civilising effect on me, given time. We made our first private-life contact not at Harmondsworth or in the Kombibus but at the London Library in St James's Square. I was there doing research into authors' photographs. Each week I gave myself a whole day at the London Library to dig up previously unused, easily distinguishable pictures of, say, Maxwell Anderson, Sherwood Anderson and Robert E. Sherwood. This took about twenty minutes. The rest of the day I would read. I read many volumes of the proceedings of the Nuremberg Tribunal, thereby saddening myself deeply but gaining a valuable inoculation of disillusionment – the precondition for a realistic happiness. Just on cue to help me test this theory out, Leslie showed up in one of the metal-floored book-stacks so that I could clank casually around the corner of a wall of shelves and meet her face to face. She was collecting references for one of the Peregrines she was editing. Peregrines were seriously highbrow Penguins and Leslie was a seriously highbrow person. Being that, being a woman and being in publishing, she was also seriously underpaid, but her little basement flat in Pimlico was a delight. Well used to not noticing my surroundings, I noticed these. Like everything about her the interior decoration was lightly done but not too dimity. There were postcard pictures of Colette and Simone de Beauvoir, of Alma Mahler-Werfel and Lou Andreas-Salomé. Not even names to me at that time, they crowded Leslie's mantelpiece with what she presumably took to be friendly faces. Virginia Woolf was up there on the wall, like a sad horse sticking its head in through a window. Sipping tea, I made myself at home. Helping myself to her vodka, I made myself too at home, but that didn't matter at first. The bull had arrived in the china shop but the proprietress welcomed the diversion.

A lot went on in two weeks. With Robin either out of town or safely ironing a large pile of shirts, I took Leslie to see the newly reconstituted complete print of *La Règle du jeu* at the Academy. She knew much more about Renoir than I did but imparted the knowledge more mercifully than I would have done had the positions been reversed. She had read modern languages at Somerville and had a wall full of Pléiade and Insel Verlag thin-paper editions to prove it. I scanned their immaculate spines with the mixture of desire and fury with which I still look at closed books even today. Eight years had gone by since she had come down from Oxford but she still went there every second weekend. The name Geoffrey was mentioned. I imagined some weedy countertenor in a long black academic gown. Casting myself as the iconoclast – it didn't take much effort – I trampled on her tentatively expressed nostalgia for the cloisters, the libraries and the crocus-bordered lawns. In view of the fact that I was heading for just such a haven myself, this was the yelping of a dog in the manger, but it jolted her from her melancholy. During tea at the Tate one Saturday afternoon I gave her my complete diagnosis of Britain's post-imperial ills. In the setting of Rex Whistler's light-fantastic murals, my oration must have sounded wonderfully incongruous. Certainly it got her attention. Resting her chin on those porcelain wrists she stared at me absorbed, as if Lenin had mounted a soap-box in Kew Gardens.

Since I was too young for her in every way, the law of diminishing returns would have set in eventually, but for the nonce she was not bored. Horrified, but not bored. What put her off, then? Perhaps it was a combination of things, tolerable as separate symptoms yet adding up to a syndrome that no woman of refinement could long countenance. My nicotine-gilded right hand might have been a drawcard on its own: the man with the golden arm. Smoke must have given my lank hair and beard a cosy smell, like the snug of an old pub. My British hamburger breath spoke challengingly of the modern Britain. Hush Puppies having attained a ubiquity which made me less defiant about associating them with the repressive footwear of the sahibs, I had bought a pair, saving money by choosing a brand called something else. Judging by how, after the first hour of having had them on, the sweat of my feet reacted with their unbreathing uppers, my new shoes should have been called Mush Puppies. After a week they were Slush Puppies. Yet Leslie was able to laugh about them as I left them outside in the area under the wrought-iron staircase.

What she couldn't laugh at, however, was the way I started turning up half-cut as soon as I thought she was in the bag, and then getting fully cut while I was with her. She might have pointed out, correctly, that it was an insult. Instead she just drifted out of reach. Before I could wake up to what was going missing, our friendship was back to where it began. I supposed then, and still prefer to suppose now, that I wanted it that way, and so hurried the business to its conclusion. There is, of course, always the possibility, however vanishingly small, that she simply didn't like me, but that sort of thing happens only to other men, doesn't it? No, she was too serious, too intense, too honest, too much. After my first evening with her I was already writing poems about saying good-bye for ever. It was a bit of a blow to find out that she felt roughly the same way, yet hurt pride was lost in the relief. Writers much more exalted than I am have the same weakness. Think twice before you get mixed up with a writer, and ten times before you marry one. Writers want things to be over, so that they can write the elegy. Gray toured that churchyard on the run.

18

Prelude to the Aftermath

You could tell how winter became spring by the way the pile of manuscript paper representing *The Charge of the Light Fandango* doubled in size, from two pages to four pages. There had never been four pages to match them. Spencer and I had once written obscurely but here was the evidence that we had grown out of all that. Now we wrote impenetrably. We were producing the first truly post-Cubist material in the history of comedy. Any idea that made us laugh we would hone and refine until it didn't. Then we would try it on Pam to make sure that it met our standards. If she looked sufficiently bewildered, it was in. If she laughed, we took it back for a rewrite.

Despite the unnerving proximity of the lost Leslie, I was also feeling pretty cocky at work. Sir Allen Lane had given over the day-to-day management of Penguin to a whizz-kid called Tony Godwin. Actually Godwin was already in his forties but it was a symptom of Britain's post-war condition that anyone given power before his hair turned white was called a whizz-kid. Godwin's hair was worn long and thick to frame his Caribbean sun-tan, with a candy-striped high-collared shirt, kipper tie and waist-hugging charcoal mohair suit all conspiring to connect the heavy head with the lightweight shoes. A star player in a gentlemen's game, Godwin was clearly very bright. His neglect of the back catalogue was to have deleterious effects in the long term, but there were enough attendant lords who could have looked after that aspect if they had seen its urgency. In the search for new titles, however, he was truly adventurous. He brought in a young editor called Tony Richardson – no relation to the film director – who took the unprecedented step of commissioning a book about the Beatles. I liked Richardson's company. More surprisingly, since he was so fastidiously quiet, he liked mine, and over coffee in the canteen would take time to explain his concern with trivia. Instead of dismissing popularity as a sure sign of the meretricious, he wanted to find out what lay behind it. Laden with first-class academic honours, he was properly suspicious of mere trendiness – the word was new then – but equally averse to the ivory tower, which he thought was a dead weight. The energy of the ignorant fascinated him. He was a deep young man but it turned out, alas, that a lot of his reticence was economy of effort. He was ill, and soon died. Hardly having known him, I missed him, and some people who knew him better never quite got over the loss.

So the two big ideas I had discussed with Richardson I took to Godwin himself. Penguin had published the occasional science fiction novel in the worthy British tradition but there were vast American sources which remained untapped. There was a boom on the way and Penguin could get in first. The same applied to books about the movies – not boring studies by Paul Rotha about Film or Cinema, but books about the movies. I wrote Godwin a long memo on the subject. To his credit he took me out to lunch on the strength of it. I must have put my case badly. Proving to him that I was a fanatic in both fields was probably a mistake. Dismissing his driver and taking the wheel of the big Jaguar himself, he drove us to a secluded pub. Seizing my opportunity before he got the car into third gear, I spoke continuously, but instead of raving about twenty different science fiction writers with names like Cordwainer Simak and swooning over twenty different film directors with names like Ray Siodmak, I should have been judiciously enthusiastic about a maximum two of each. 'We might do a bit more science fiction,' Godwin said, in a tone of voice that told me my cause was lost, 'but I don't need a buff who knows all about the neglected minor novels of Kohl and Pornbluth. I need an editor who can see a big project all the way through without wasting my time and the company's money.' Dandyish himself, he perhaps took my beard as a sign of unsoundness. He would have been right, of course. 'Pohl and Kornbluth,' I said feebly, knowing that he had slipped up on purpose as a contribution towards letting me down lightly. Still, the pub lunch had made a change from the canteen. In the canteen I would have had a tray full of ordinary food and some excellent views of Leslie. In the pub I got a piece of stale French loaf with a dead shallot laid out on it, a dollop of shepherd's pie like a rhino's diarrhoea, and a good solid dose of rejection. By and large it is our failures that civilise us, but one doesn't want to take that principle too far.

Up until that point I had taken a relaxed attitude to my job, but from then on I became positively somnolent. With the arrival of spring it became easier to get a good day's sleep just by resting my head on the desk. Come autumn I would be back in those groves of academe outside of which, it was becoming increasingly clear, I was unqualified to function. Meanwhile there was one last summer of hard labour to be lived through. The *vie bohème* at Melbury Road reached its peak, and, as usually occurs when happiness is perceived as such, began instantly to melt away. On weekends we drank at Henekey's in the Portobello Road. Ella Fitzgerald sang at the Hammersmith Odeon. Callas and Gobbi were in *Tosca* at Covent Garden. Not even Nick Thesinger could get in but we all saw the show on television, which was black and white in those days but made Callas look all the more dramatic. The girls on the top floor had a television set that gave you quite a good picture if you hit it with your clenched fist at the right angle. I spent hours in front of it and would have been hard put to disagree with anyone who accused me of wasting my time. Only a decade later did it turn out that I had been engaged in formative studies.

As a luxury we would dine out at Jimmy's in Soho. Jimmy's was a basement restaurant in Frith Street. Bianchi's, the restaurant favoured by successful people in journalism and television – not yet collectively known as the media – was further along the street and two floors up. It was said that those two floors were the longest climb in London. It cost more than ten times as much to eat at Bianchi's as at Jimmy's and I liked things well enough below ground. The place had started life as an air-raid shelter but had gone down since. Yet the low price of the lamb chops was not reflected in their taste, which was made only more piquant by the number and size of the caterpillars in the salad. On Sunday afternoons, with attendant women reading heavy newspapers on the sidelines, we played soccer with a tennis ball in Holland Park, adding our profane cries to the clattering of the peacocks who otherwise carried the full burden of disrupting the open-air concerts.

Reg went missing from the team when he got a message from Sydney saying that an ex girl-friend had died after an illegal operation. Though it was nothing to do with him, he blamed himself for having been away, a reaction which suggested – correctly, as things turned out – that he would be going home for good. In those last pre-Pill days, the possibility of a back-street abortion was the unstated but inescapable sub-text of the revels, whether you were a shy tyro in Sydney or an experienced roué in London. One of the girls upstairs at Melbury Road was caught out during my last few weeks in residence. Her

English company director suitor was long gone. I got the job of taking her to the appointment, waiting for her in the dark parlour which served as a reception area, and taking her home when the deed was done. Her sense of loss afterwards would have been food for the moralist. Yet what struck me, and strikes me still, was her fear beforehand. I wish I could have said better things. Thank God for changed times. The contraceptives weren't hard to live with if a lady didn't mind playing hostess to a small floppy frisbee full of hair-gel and a gentleman didn't mind dressing part of his anatomy as a bleached frogman. But a misfortune could bring misery. The way out of the misery could bring tragedy. Women took that way out because the alternatives were impossible. Today people need to be reminded that the choice is not between legal abortion and the supposedly edifying effects of bringing up an unwanted child. The choice is between legal abortion and illegal abortion. To know something of what an illegal abortion was like, you didn't need to have seen a girl's corpse after an unsuccessful operation. All you needed to have seen was a girl's face on the way to a successful one. They never put the appointment in their diaries. They always wrote the address on a piece of paper, so that they could throw it away afterwards.

Society was to blame. Actually, on this point, it was, but I held it to blame on most other points as well. My radicalism, now further fuelled by semi-regular reading of the *New Left Review*, found expression at the London School of Economics, where I turned up unasked to the weekly student debates and joined in from the floor. The standard of articulacy was not high. Neither was my standard of logic, but that deficiency made me more prolix instead of less. Harry Pollitt's son Brian, an ex-President of the Cambridge Union, was the star guest one night. He had inherited his father's politics but a privileged education had obviously softened them. When my turn came to speak I pointed out, truly if not wisely, that egalitarianism would remain a dream as long as places like Cambridge existed. Pollitt agreed that Cambridge should be levelled forthwith but put in a plea for the retention of King's College Chapel. He had his tongue in his cheek and knew it. I had my head up my arse and didn't, but to some of the less perspicacious students present I must have sounded like the more committed revolutionary. After the debate, two of them approached me and told me proudly that while earning extra money on the building site of a new housing development they had been deliberately fiddling with the wiring so as to hasten the downfall of capitalism. With sudden visions of some old lady switching on the immersion heater and blasting herself to kingdom come, I instructed these teenage saboteurs to get down there next morning and put things right pronto. Shivering in the summer midnight as I waited for a bus back to Kensington High Street, I resolved to abandon the revolution then and there. This might sound like easy come, easy go. But I doubt if I was ever the sort of harebrained dabbler with ideas who turns up in Dostoevsky and Conrad. My convictions were strong enough. Yet my instincts were even stronger, and they were all against any notion that ends can justify means. I had what it took to be feckless, but *realpolitik* was beyond me. So it needed only a little event to overcome a big idea. Many reluctant liberals would have similar tales to tell about their retreat from radical certainty. There is no mystery involved. The solidarity of the Left is a mirage. The common ground between revolutionaries and parliamentarians is made of air. Its transparency can be rendered apparent by a very small fact. You can be in a demonstration, someone near you will bend to pick up a stone, and you will realise that you are in the wrong place. Being obliged to remember from that day forward that your fine ideas weighed less than a pebble will never be comforting, but always salutary.

Not having yet informed Penguin that I would soon be

doing a bunk, I shamelessly took my annual holiday as a reward for all my hard work. Françoise was waiting on Florence railway station and her joy at seeing my beard again can be imagined. This time there was no question of compromising her reputation at the *pensione*. Instead we took a room at Lastra a Signa, a suburb on the edge of town, where I compromised her reputation with the entire district. The room was an ex-bathroom which had been converted by adding extra tiles to the ceiling. The landlady made it clear that only the recent double hernia sustained by her hod-carrying husband had led her to even consider offering this wonderful abode to an unmarried couple. Unlike her husband, however, she had the forbearance not to join the crowd of menacingly staring locals who followed us in the street. Usually he was in the forefront, no doubt to make up with persecuting zeal for the compromise which had been forced on his wife by his economic weakness. For a man with a serious physical disability he certainly knew how to spit. It was like that terrible scene in *L'Avventura* when Monica Vitti gets followed around by a town's whole population of deprived males. Françoise's good looks, however, though sufficiently startling, were not quite enough to explain the element of potential homicide informing that massed masculine gaze. It was my beard that had tipped them over the edge. They probably didn't like my shoes, either – a new ox-blood pair with gold buckles at the sides. The shoes had cost not much more than five pounds, so I don't suppose the buckles were real gold. But they weren't superfluous. They were holding down the straps. It was the straps that were superfluous.

Incipient hatred of all Italian males was staved off by deeper acquaintance with Leopardi and Enrico. Leopardi had been dead for some time but his poetry, painfully construed by me with Françoise's patient assistance, was a revelation. Enrico's paintings perhaps lacked the same hard-won authority but he was alive. He was the lover of Françoise's friend Faith, a fine-boned English modern languages graduate who had come to Florence in search of Petrarch and stayed on to live with Enrico. They had a farmhouse on a winding road out past Fiesole in the northern hills. Enrico helped buy the food for Faith to cook. He also helped cook it. He had a *boules* court set up in the back yard, near the chicken coop. His Italian was fast and funny yet so clear that I could feel my grasp of the language improving as I listened. He spent a lot of time on helping me to speak it – far more time than any truly committed artist would have had to spare. The truth was that his temporary job as an art teacher was becoming a full-time job and that both he and Faith had fallen victim to happiness. Instead of achieving their ambitions, they had improved their lives. It was all such a waste, I would tell them as I drank their wine. Françoise agreed with this analysis, or anyway didn't disagree.

Back in England, I found Dalziel on the point of leaving for Africa. A job as head of the Nigerian Government Film Unit had come up and he had decided that a couple of years spent making a documentary every two weeks about politicians giving speeches would still be better experience than living on hope in London. The rough cut of *The Man from the Organisation* got him the job. The Nigerians thought it was a true story but liked the close-ups. I hated to see him go, but in only a few days I would be gone myself. Dibbs had already left for New York, where his sequence of paintings featuring Delish on a massage table had created a sensation. The masseur was variously Freud, Einstein, Kafka and Elvis Presley, with appended texts from each. Dave shared my scepticism but characteristically cut through to the heart of the matter. 'If he spent less time writing down quotable quotes he could learn to draw,' said the new head of the Nigerian Government Film Unit while packing his canvas hold-all. 'But he's got the colour. Especially that sky blue. It looks just like home.' Warning me not to get lost in the books, Dalziel moved out. His parting words were typically lyrical. 'Don't put a dent in the beef bayonet.' Until three replacements moved in I had the flat to myself. At Penguin I had given my notice, which was eagerly accepted. Leslie seemed to mind least of all. They would have been even keener to see my back if they had known how close I had come to supplying Bertram D. Wolfe's photograph for the cover of a book by Bernard Wolfe. At least I hadn't sent them Virginia Woolf. But only a frantic sprint down the corridor and a degrading last-minute tussle with the art-editor had averted the same sort of catastrophe which I had been hired to prevent in the first place.

Down at the Iron Bridge I told Dingo all about it as part of a campaign to amuse him on his last night. Unaccountably he had decided that the place to be an Australian journalist was Australia, so he was not attempting to renew his appointment. He told me all this through the din caused by an ancient male singer who upgraded his performance of 'Mule Train' by hitting himself on the head with a tin tray. Not notably more smashed than usual, Dingo sold me the Ford Popular for a shilling. A non-driver, I didn't want it for transport. I wanted it for a monument. By dead of night, Dingo steered it to the designated spot, and there we left it to rust – in front of Hearty McHale's. The first phase of my career in London was thus summed up as having had nuisance value and nothing more. I went home to an empty flat.

My suitcase looked eager to be away. Stained white with dried rain, even my shoes were itching to be gone. By now they were Gush Puppies, but they would take me to safety. On the flag-stones of ancient courtyards they would find a sure footing.